NOT to be taken into the air

"Tee Emm is for Official Use Only. This means it must only be read by those for whom it is intended. No part of it must be published and nothing it contains must be told or written to anyone who might publish it. And, of course, it must not be taken into the air".

the life and times of
PILOT OFFICER
PRUNE

BEING
THE OFFICIAL STORY OF

TEE EMM

WRITTEN & DESIGNED BY
TIM HAMILTON

HISTORICAL ADVISER
CHARLES W. CAIN

LONDON: HMSO

Text and book design Copyright Tim Hamilton-Ayres.

First published HMSO 1991.

ISBN 0 11 772629 X

HMSO publications are available from:

HMSO Publications Centre
(Mail and telephone orders only)
PO Box 276, London, SW8 5DT
Telephone orders 071–873 9090
General enquiries 071–873 0011
(queuing system in operation for both numbers)

HMSO Bookshops
49 High Holborn, London, WC1V 6HB   071–873 0011 (counter service only)
258 Broad Street, Birmingham, B1 2HE   021–643 3740
Southey House, 33 Wine Street, Bristol, BS1 2BQ   (0272) 264306
9–21 Princess Street, Manchester, M60 8AS   061–834 7201
80 Chichester Street, Belfast, BT1 4JY   (0232) 238451
71 Lothian Road, Edinburgh, EH3 9AZ   031–228 4181

HMSO's Accredited Agents
(see Yellow Pages)
and through good booksellers

Printed in the United Kingdom for HMSO
Dd 0290196 3/91 C50 6936 12521

CONTENTS

ACKNOWLEDGEMENTS

It is appropriate to express my sincere thanks to all those Individuals and Institutions whose records, personal remembrances and time created the backbone for this book. Orchestrated jointly by Charles W. Cain and myself, the research work would not have been possible without the help of the following: First and foremost Mrs A.A. Willis, Anthony Armstrong's wife; Anthony Armstrong's daughter Felicity Barnett and her brother Humphrey Willis; The Public Record Office, Kew; Group Captain S. 'Sammy' Wroath; Flight Lieutenant Adrian Bishop; Robert C. Osborn and Sandy Russel of US Naval Aviation News; Peter Endsleigh Castle; Colonel Bernard Duperier FAFL, Paris; The Royal Aeronautical Society and Air Commodore David Lawrence and Andrew Renwick of the RAF Museum, Hendon. In addition, many individuals have helped by providing information in their specialist fields or from their personal experiences or have helped by pointing in the right direction and they also deserve my gratitude: Air Commodore J. Leathart; Professor Samuel Hynes, USMC (USA); Flight Lieutenant A. Boysons; W.B. Klepacki (Poland); C.F. Shores; J. Meaden; Warrant Officer R. Ellis; Flight Lieutenant C. Beasley; Hans H. Oerke (Germany); Dr D.J. Voaden (USA); D. Birch (Rolls-Royce); J. Goulding and N.B. Wiltshire (Australia). On the visual aspects I have to thank Peter Endsleigh Castle again, John Camm for his time and effort, Terence J. Donovan for his photographic help and Trent Nicholson at Graphic Examples for the computer make-up. Encouragement is an important factor in producing a book and here I would like to thank both Phillip Brooks and Keith Riley at HMSO. I would also like to thank the Ministry of Defence Air Historical Branch (RAF) for the guidance they have provided and Eric Munday who has carefully checked the manuscript. Last but not least I would like to thank Charles W. Cain for his untiring efforts in both research and in checking my final draft both for errors of ignorance and consistency.

DEDICATED TO

The memory of my father,
Warrant Officer Charles 'Lew' Ayres
of Nos 84, 27 and 217 Squadrons,
who fostered my imagination with tales of
his exploits and who gave me my love of flying.

and for

MICHÈLE and ALEXANDRA.

The first full drawing of 'Tee Emm's' protagonist.

INTRODUCTION

Brought up against a Royal Air Force background with a father who saw Aircrew service in Iraq, the North-West Frontier and World War Two, I first became aware of an 'RAF Character' as a scribbled drawing of a pilot with a plum nose and a dog, executed on the back of an envelope for my childish amusement. His name, his role and its significance to RAF history eluded me for some thirty or so years until a colleague, the Historical Adviser of this book, brought him to my attention as a largely forgotten element of RAF training strategy. On first being shown copies of 'Tee Emm' I realised what a rich source of material had lain fallow (largely because of its 'Official Use Only' classification). Further research in remaining Air Ministry files, discussions with many ex-RAF Aircrew and access, courtesy of Mrs A.A. Willis, to the private papers of Anthony Armstrong, convinced me that, together with the original illustrations in 'Tee Emm', a book was in the making.

The difficulty was knowing how far and how deep to go, since a lot of the material published was of a semi-technical nature and would demand a certain knowledge of aviation. Rather, I decided to relate 'Tee Emm', and its principal protaganist, to the ongoing needs of the RAF during World War Two by extracting from Anthony Armstrong's texts, and by carefully selecting illustrations, to paint a picture which could be set against a modicum of historical background. All in all, there were some 48 different artists who drew for 'Tee Emm' but only one writer. The fact that Anthony Armstrong persistently used the royal 'We' throughout the 60 monthly issues suitably disguises that fact. Aided by a staff of two, and latterly three (mention should be made here of WAAF Section Officer 'Copper' and Warrant Officer J.H. Lea) plus Bill Hooper as staff artist, Armstrong's output was prolific especially since he was very often working in subject areas in which he possessed no knowledge. The development of the character 'Pilot Officer Prune' no doubt aided this process since it allowed Anthony Armstrong cleverly to deflect hard-hitting points onto a mythical scapegoat and let the sentiment 'If the cap fits wear it' ride along. 'Tee Emm' and 'Prune' were inseparable and although this fictitious Pilot Officer was posted throughout the various Commands, Anthony Armstrong treated him as though he were a correspondent in the field. This technique met with the instant approval of RAF Aircrew, the humour and the ideology reflecting the true spirit of the RAF in World War Two - as it still does some 50 years later.

Tim Hamilton

IN THE BEGINNING

Prune P., Pilot Officer, No.89008, Fictional Person, RAF for the use of, was not the product of any sudden inspiration but rather the result of an evolution of ideas. Although the 1st of April 1941 marked his adoption as an official character in the Royal Air Force, with the blessing of everyone from the Secretary of State for Air downwards, he had been in gestation for some many months and the concept can be traced back to 1938. Assen Jordanoff, an Officer in the Bulgarian Air Force of World War I, had emigrated to the USA in the early 'twenties where he established himself in the aircraft industry as a draughtsman, engineer and as an occasional flying instructor. By 1930 he had turned his attention to aviation journalism and, utilising his vast fund of experience, decided to fill what he saw as a vacuum in the market for Flying Training Manuals. Jordanoff's first book, 'Your Wings', popularised a down-to-earth approach to grasping the technicalities of flying without trivialising the seriousness of flight safety. It was heralded as a breakthrough in training manuals and, spurred-on by its success, Jordanoff set about writing 'Through the Overcast', a manual on instrument flying. To help him reinforce various points, he created a character called 'Cloudy Joe' (illustrated opposite) who, like a ventriloquist's dummy, could make outrageous statements encompassing key aspects of flight safety – thus introducing cautionary humour into an essentially serious subject. Drawn by Fred L. Meager, 'Cloudy Joe' was described by Jordanoff as having a physical appearance that reflected his state of mind. "He is enthusiastic and eager to learn, but I am afraid he will never be anything but a blunderer. Yet I am grateful to him, for he has taught me how a number of things ought *not* to be done". 'Through the Overcast' was followed by 'Safety in Flight'. By the early 'forties the three titles had been bulk-purchased for official use by the Air Forces of the USA, Canada, Britain and the USSR, with more than 400,000 copies circulating in military training centres.

Quality of aircrew training had always been a keynote of Royal Air Force policy but by early 1940 it was realised that the dramatic expansion of the RAF, vital to a successful outcome in the war with Germany, could severely compromise even the most basic of requirements. Beaverbrook had been given charge of the new Ministry of Aircraft Production and, by cutting red-tape, was boosting the numbers of aircraft available to meet the predicted targets. The Air Council had already, with infinite wisdom, inaugurated the EATS (Empire Air Training Scheme) to operate in the Dominions. This scheme was primarily designed to produce personnel trained to a standard of competence but still lacking final training in tactics and on operational 'type'. Although EATS would take a certain strain off the RAF, training still remained uppermost in the Air Council's mind. At a meeting in June 1940, it was decided to create the new position of Air Member for Training to draw together the various elements. Air Vice-Marshal A.G.R. Garrod, OBE, MC, DFC, was duly promoted to Air Marshal and appointed to AMT with the brief to create three Directorates, Flying, Technical and Operational, under which all aspects of RAF training could be commanded. His appointment coincided with the defeat of the BAFF (British Air Forces in France) and Churchill's chilling warning that the Battle of France had been lost and the Battle for Britain was about to begin – and Garrod knew he had a massive task ahead with EATS not yet due to be effective. The problem that was continually to plague him was Operational Training. It was one thing to produce suitably air-experienced crew but another to impart the experience learned in front-line fighting; in addition to which the Battle of Britain demanded that every experienced Pilot be held at 'Readiness'. There was simply no time to devote to a young replacement with only a few hours on type. Reserve Squadrons had been designated to fill the role but they in turn were called forward. As the Battle of Britain drew to a successful close, AM Garrod realised that an extensive review of Operational Training, extending even into fully operational Squadrons, was going to be necessary.

After France and before the Battle – 54 Squadron at Hornchurch.

Anthony Armstrong at work in his study.

By the late autumn of 1940 plans were being laid to create a series of Operational Training Units under the direct control of each of three Commands, Fighter, Bomber and Coastal; and Senior Officers in the AMT's Office had been studying various ideas to speed-up the training programme. Trainees were to be instructed by fully operational personnel, attached to these Units for 'rest periods', attaining a further 40 hours of flying time over a period of four-to-six weeks before being posted. It was obvious that this time, which was as much as the RAF could afford, would never be totally adequate and 'front-line experience' could only really be learnt at first hand. There was also an argument that 'front-line crew' should themselves undergo an element of retraining to keep up-to-scratch and iron-out bad habits. Finally it was agreed to opt for a regular distribution of information which would impart knowledge from the more experienced to the less; and also act as a reminder to those who had 'put some time in', without seeming to preach or labour the point. This was to become 'Training Memoranda' and some discussion was given over to deciding the form it should take. Demonstrably, the Americans had achieved great success in using a light-hearted approach and it was agreed that a mild use of humour which, after all, had a tradition in the RAF, might ensure that the information was read and remembered. To produce such a regular monthly publication was beyond the capability of anyone currently attached to the AMT's Office. It would require an expert in humorous writing and Wing Commander H.V. Satterly ventured a suggestion.

Before his posting to the Directorate of Operational Training at the Air Ministry in Kingsway, Satterly had been with the Department of War Tactics and Training (absorbed into the AMT's Office) based at Harrow. At that time, with a dozen or so Officers, he was sharing a house in Hendon, "owned by Handley Page who had lent it for the purpose". One of these was a certain Lieutenant Colonel J.C.T. Willis of the Royal Engineers on 'loan' to the Air Ministry Map Department at the Deputy Directorate of Intelligence. His brother, Major A.A. Willis, MC, Royal Engineers and recently retired from the Reserve List, was better known as Anthony Armstrong, the author, playwright and humorist 'A.A.' of 'Punch'. The opportunity was too good to miss and Harold Satterly approached 'Chris' Willis (as he was known to his friends) to sound out his advice. Anthony Armstrong was busy heading up his local division of the Home Guard near the

Flight Lieutenant A.A. Willis in conference with the AMT.

family house in East Harting, West Sussex, as well as completing a book 'We Like the Country' and writing his contributions to 'Punch'. 'Chris' Willis thought that Anthony, much to Satterly's delight, would jump at the opportunity to do something for his country in which he could use his real talent. The result was that, with unheard of haste, Anthony Armstrong was summoned to London to meet Air Commodore A.J. Capel, the then Director of the Directorate of Operational Training. Inside a week he had been offered a Commission in the RAF Volunteer Reserve and was posted to the AMT's Office with the responsibility of producing a regular monthly magazine on a subject about which he knew nothing.

After passing a medical, in which he managed to convince the Doctor he had no intention of flying, and receiving the third degree at a Selection Board for what was supposed to be a 'rubber stamp job',

Anthony Armstrong found himself ensconced in an office at Princes House, Kingsway, with the rank of Pilot Officer (but designated Acting Flight Lieutenant) and being told to get on with it. The outline document with which he was presented comprised a series of close-typed Roneo-ed foolscap sheets, frequently not very legible and written in turgid 'Whitehallese'. His brief was to produce a. layout and sample of the proposed publication for AM Garrod to present at Air Council by mid-January 1941. It was already December 1940 and Anthony Armstrong was unsure where to start. "After wondering for a while about my new baby – for the appellation 'Training Memorandum' was enough to sink a battleship – I found myself idly jotting on my blotting paper, just to see how it looked, the initials spelt in full – 'Tee Emm' and I knew I was on my way". Assistance, particularly with the complicated nature of some of the material and with a vital Air Force feel, was forthcoming in

13

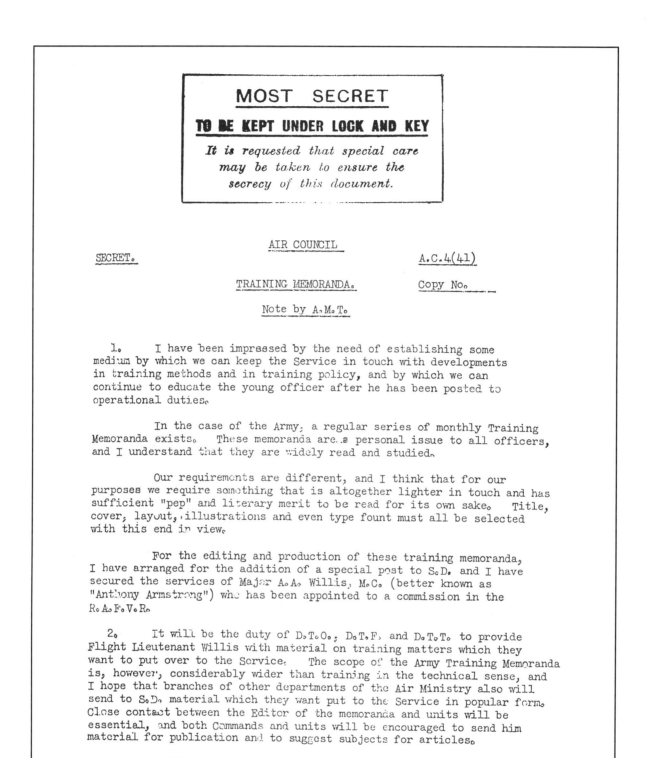

AIR COUNCIL

SECRET.   A.C.4(41)

TRAINING MEMORANDA.   Copy No. ____

Note by A.M.T.

1.   I have been impressed by the need of establishing some
medium by which we can keep the Service in touch with developments
in training methods and in training policy, and by which we can
continue to educate the young officer after he has been posted to
operational duties.

        In the case of the Army, a regular series of monthly Training
Memoranda exists.   These memoranda are a personal issue to all officers,
and I understand that they are widely read and studied.

        Our requirements are different, and I think that for our
purposes we require something that is altogether lighter in touch and has
sufficient "pep" and literary merit to be read for its own sake.   Title,
cover, layout, illustrations and even type fount must all be selected
with this end in view.

        For the editing and production of these training memoranda,
I have arranged for the addition of a special post to S.D. and I have
secured the services of Major A.A. Willis, M.C. (better known as
"Anthony Armstrong") who has been appointed to a commission in the
R.A.F.V.R.

2.   It will be the duty of D.T.O., D.T.F, and D.T.T. to provide
Flight Lieutenant Willis with material on training matters which they
want to put over to the Service.   The scope of the Army Training Memoranda
is, however, considerably wider than training in the technical sense, and
I hope that branches of other departments of the Air Ministry also will
send to S.D. material which they want put to the Service in popular form.
Close contact between the Editor of the memoranda and units will be
essential, and both Commands and units will be encouraged to send him
material for publication and to suggest subjects for articles.

        I will bring to the Air Council meeting a note by Flight
Lieutenant Willis outlining his proposals for the first number of
"Tee Emm", and I hope that the Council will be willing to give general
approval to my proposal and also to the form and layout of the publication.

the shape of Pilot Officer John Duckworth Irving, OBE, MC – and Wing Commander L.H. 'Joe' Stewart from the Directorate of Technical Training. Using some of his contacts to provide illustrations, Anthony Armstrong rapidly set to work creating the final form that 'Tee Emm' was going to take. 'Fougasse', Cyril Kenneth Bird (of 'Careless Talk Costs Lives' fame), designed a cover in RAF blue, instead of the usual offical pale buff, with the Air Force eagle wearing spectacles and reading-up 'gen' from a book. AM Garrod liked what he saw and on the 18th of January 1941 he presented a report together with Anthony Armstrong's proposals for Air Council approval.

A 'Met' lecture at Elementary Flying Training School.

That AM Garrod had already won Air Council support for his ideas there is very little doubt, for the publication that he proposed was extraordinary in RAF terms. Humour had been used in Flight Safety posters but serious areas like training were another thing. Furthermore, AM Garrod suggested that there be no committees to look over 'Tee Emm'; the Editor should be given a free hand, "and change him if he fails to deliver the goods," he added in his report. It was suggested that regular monthly publication "should be in the 'Official Use Only' category and distributed to all Officers of the General Duties Branch who had passed out of their Operational Training Unit, with an additional distribution to Officers' Messes and to crew rooms to cover airman pilots, observers and wireless operator/air gunners." There is no record of any misgivings and 'Tee Emm', with Anthony Armstrong at the helm, was given the green light, and he was instructed to proceed as soon as possible. It was one thing to put together a proposal but quite another to set up for regular production. An editorial assistant needed to be appointed, printers had to be organised and a bank of contributions needed to be built up from which materials could be selected. A target date was set for the first issue of the 1st of April 1941. This must have pleased Anthony Armstrong (and he probably had some hand in deciding it) for April Fool's Day was not only the perfect day to launch a humorous magazine but it was also the RAF's birthday.

Although the style of 'Tee Emm' had been agreed, it was still entirely up to Anthony Armstrong as to how he chose to apply humour to the various subjects. 'Joe' Stewart pressed Armstrong to create a single character which could provide a running theme and be used to present points-of-view. He was well aware of Assen Jordanoff's 'Cloudy Joe' and suggested that 'Tee Emm' should have its own

Wing Commander 'Joe' Stewart by 'Wren'.

15

Various artists known to Anthony Armstrong were called on to illustrate specific points.

'duff' pilot. Anthony Armstrong liked the idea of using a character to show how *not* to do something and it would be easier to deflect humour off a fictitious personality. Armstrong also had a reputation for such characters in his long-running series of humorous Army books, including the recently published 'Warriors at War' – in which he had created such stalwarts as 'Major Saddleflap'

and 'Corporal Pullthrough'. Stewart suggested that the RAF's character be anonymous and non-attributable to any serving member but nevertheless familiar enough for everyone to feel they knew him. The question of name followed rank. He had to be the lowest level of commission, since 'Tee Emm' was predominantly aimed at Officers, and his name had to be simple, representing the very nature of his personality. 'Pilot Officer Prune' came instantly to mind; 'Prune' had been used to describe an affable idiot for some decades and was popular among the public schoolboys of the 'thirties, many of whom were now in the RAF. It also had a sense of the ridiculous since Dickens teamed it with 'prisms' in 'Little Dorrit'. For Anthony Armstrong, the alliterative quality was too good to resist and he added the initial 'P' for 'Percival' which he had previously used as a suitable name for a 'dunderhead'. Shortened to Pilot Officer Percy Prune, Anthony Armstrong handed this new-found character his own personal Service number and set to launch him on an unsuspecting Royal Air Force as though he really existed.

Hitherto Anthony Armstrong had planned to use illustrations to uplift certain articles; with specific 'cartoons' drawn either for humour's sake or to make a point. Illustrations would be by various artists/illustrators, some of whom he had already worked with and others whom he knew through his connections with 'Punch' and the 'Savage Club'. He had already received some such illustrations for the first issue (illustration left) and was loath to drop the idea. But if Pilot Officer Prune was to be launched successfully, he would have to be depicted and this needed continuity. What was needed was to find someone who could give a regular commitment to 'Tee Emm' for the duration of the publication and that could mean possibly for the War. The few drawings required each month could not justify someone being recruited for the Volunteer Reserve. Anthony Armstrong discussed the problem with his friend, the cartoonist David Langdon, who was himself already heavily committed. There was also the question of what Prune should look like. Talk had been of giving him a handlebar moustache but argument had gone against that as being too much of a cliche and a more expressionless face would lend him open to interpretation. Certainly he was to be scruffy but only just enough to exaggerate the already relaxed dress of the Battle of Britain 'Fighter Boys'. Anthony Armstrong needed to find someone and to find him fast. All the Services produced artists

'Forget-Me-Nots For Fighters' although a slim book of just 44 pages was elaborately produced – printed on good quality paper with a gold blocked design on its blue cloth hard-backed binding. Designed very much with the fresh young Pilot in mind its last two pages, under the heading personalities, were designed for 'sharp' observations and comments plus autographs from other Pilots in the Squadron.

and the RAF was no exception so, utilising the 'grapevine' extending from the AMT's Office, he put out a search for someone to draw Prune. Within days a copy of 'Forget-Me-Nots For Fighters' had been placed on his desk.

At the same time that Anthony Armstrong had been trying to explain to the Selection Board why the RAF urgently needed a playwright, Air Vice-Marshal R.E. Saul, Air Officer Commanding No.13 Group in the North, was busy preparing a Training Book based on the lessons learned by Pilots who had fought in the Battle of Britain. Apart from its defensive duties, 13 Group had become both a training ground and a rest area for those Squadrons which had been severely reduced in front-line action; and the book was aimed at the untested

replacements. One such Squadron was No.54, home-based at Hornchurch, and AVM Saul consulted with its Commanding Officer, Squadron Leader R.F. Boyd, over a series of 'hints and tips' (a similar idea had been published by the Directorate of Air Tactics in June 1940) to be culled from the most experienced Pilots in the Group. These 'tips' were distilled into simple statements and it was agreed some illustrations, perhaps with a touch of humour, were needed to reinforce the message. A General Duties clerk in Boyd's Squadron, Aircraftman W.J. Hooper RAFVR, had gained a growing reputation with his cartoon drawings, some of which had been pinned up in the Duty Room and the Adjutant's Office. Boyd set Hooper to work illustrating the 'tips' and the book was finally titled 'Forget-Me-Nots For Fighters'. AVM

I hope that these Training Memoranda will be widely read and studied, since I am certain that they will help us all to improve our efficiency, not only in our training but also in operations against the enemy.

Portal.

Air Chief Marshal, Chief of the Air Staff

Saul had reason to be grateful to Boyd, for he not only steered the book through to publication but used his contacts with his former Auxiliary Squadron, No.602 'City of Glasgow', to obtain sponsorship for the small print run. The book was well received by those who obtained a copy; and Anthony Armstrong was impressed because although the drawings were essentially simple, they contained a human quality that was vital if Prune was to be successfully visualised. After showing the book to Stewart, Armstrong immediately contacted Hooper and called a meeting in London; the result of which was that he was assigned to draw Prune. Formalities still had to be sorted out but W.J. Hooper, in addition to his normal duties, was officially assigned to 'Tee Emm', as Staff Artist, with permission to travel to London whenever Anthony Armstrong needed him.

With his team in place, W. Gordon Williams as Civilian Assistant Editor, a Civil Service clerk nicknamed 'Enoch' (all 'Tee Emm' clerks were subsequently nicknamed 'Enoch'), outside cartoonists/illustrators and a newly-acquired Staff Artist, Anthony Armstrong was ready to go to press. Sir Charles Portal, Air Chief Marshal and Chief of the Air Staff, wrote a brief address (which, although modified, was carried in all following issues); and, without any blast of trumpets or any kind of special celebration, 'Tee Emm' was

In the first issue the visualisation of 'Prune' was largely restricted to thumbnail drawings.

Air Chief Marshal Sir Charles Portal.

Emm' was a huge success and considered a breath of fresh air by those for whom it was intended. That is not to say it lacked any detractors but those whose upper lips bristled at the 'Boy's Own' approach were forced to admit that, for the first time, information put out by the AMT's Office could be guaranteed to be read. By the end of six months Anthony Armstrong had broadened his approach. Prune had started to feature in many of the articles, Bill Hooper's drawings were given greater space and had become more sophisticated. In fact, Pilot Officer Prune had come to life in record time and was becoming known to all in the Air Force as the Service's affable dimwit. "Fatuously exuberant yet permanently bone-headed, he invariably made a complete muck of everything he set out to do, and was an awful warning to all potential bad or foolish fliers". Prune had indeed come alive and the word took on an added meaning when hurled in gentlemanly abuse between fellow Pilots.

launched on its target date. The first issue was conservative in its approach to humour but perhaps that is what Anthony Armstrong intended. In an opening editorial he wrote that the RAF had "a tradition of ebullience, even of unconventionality", and continued by stating that it wasn't out of keeping for 'Tee Emm' to reflect this. He did, however, err on the side of caution and concluded by pointing out that "Tee Emm in whatever form it is written, contains serious matter, the whole object of which is to help. The stuff, in short, is there". Prune rated only a few mentions and five thumbnail sketches by way of introduction; but a full-length drawing on 'Tee Emm's' final page (see page 8) was to become the standard model for all future development of the character. Underneath were the lines from which 'Tee Emm's' motto would be drawn: "Pilot-Officer Prune says – 'Take Tee Emm regularly! Prevents that Thinking feeling!' ". Anthony Armstrong need not have worried. 'Tee

Room 602 in Princes House was Prune's spiritual home and Anthony Armstrong, whose humour was wont to wander from the page, soon realised that many 'chaps' seemed to believe that Prune actually existed. So, with a true sense of the ridiculous, Armstrong decided to reward their belief by providing Prune with a desk and chair in his office, plus his name correctly lettered on a card on the door. "Naturally he was rarely found in – but even more rarely found out. Within a year I had got his name and number in the Air Ministry telephone directory. People used to ring him up and write to him and send him rude presents and come in to try and see him. My invariable answer to 'phone calls – any time up to 6.30 p.m. – was: 'Sorry, he's not back from lunch yet.' Caught out once by an indignant female who said; 'But it's not yet midday,' I had to think quickly. "Not back yet from yesterday's lunch,' I amended." Peter Endsleigh Castle, with Air Intelligence as an aircraft recognition draughtsman, was posted to SD (Special

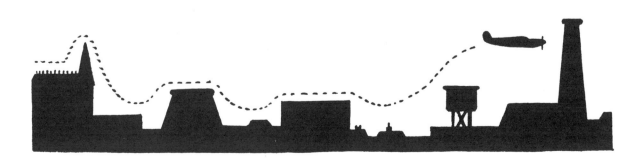

Duties) Branch at Kingsway and occupied an office along the corridor from 'Tee Emm'. "It brought a smile to my face every time I passed that room," he remembers. "Prune must have always been improperly dressed, for every time I went into Armstrong's office Prune was 'out to lunch'; but his battered cap and gasmask were always hanging there on a hatstand. And the way his desk was laid out, you'd think he'd just gone round the corner to visit the loo." (see colour plate page 86). One highlight of Prune's fictitious career came in late 1941 when an 'Efficiency Expert', conducting an investigation into what everyone actually did in the Ministry, saw Prune's name on the door and asked

Air Marshal A.G.R. Garrod.

Anthony Armstrong exactly what his job was. At first Armstrong thought he was being funny but then realised he just didn't know about Prune. So Armstrong gave him a very official-sounding synopsis of Prune's duties. It was embodied in the final Official Report to go up to the Air Council; but a Senior Clerical Officer, horrified at such subversive goings-on spotted Prune before it was too late and the Report was modified. The whole Service took Prune to its heart in a big way and most of the Ministry personnel, including Civil Servants, were proud to acknowledge his existence and would direct visitors to his office, not least AM Garrod who used him on more than one occasion to pull the legs of the uninitiated.

It may be that the reality of Prune got a little out of hand, for in the January 1942 issue of 'Tee Emm' Anthony Armstrong published a supposed letter from Pilot Officer Prune at 'RAF Station New Heary', complaining that it had come to his attention that some people were saying he was a figment of the Editor's imagination. "I gather that several people seem to have the idea that I am not a real person and that there's a suggestion that you invented me just as an imaginary character to do damfool things. I take a pretty poor view of this, I may tell you. I was posted here eight months ago

TEN LITTLE PILOT BOYS

Ten little Pilot Boys, one shot a fancy line:
  Fifth Columnists were listening and then there were nine.
Nine little Pilot Boys, one had a heavy date:
  The girl was paid by Germany and then there were eight.
Eight little Pilot Boys, one used a 'phone to Devon:
  The line was an open one and then there were seven.
Seven little Pilot Boys, one thought his drinks he'd mix:
  He talked too much when he was tight, then there were six.
Six little Pilot Boys, in a West End "dive":
  One showed off to a new-found friend, then there were five.
Five little Pilot Boys, discussing fighter lore:
  One discussed it much too loud, then there were four.
Four little Pilot Boys, one posted oversea,
  Sent a p.c. to his home, then there were three.
Three little Pilot Boys, one talked about a 'do':
  The news was passed across to France, then there were two.
Two little Pilot Boys, eager for some fun:
  One spoke about his next day job, then there was one.
One little Pilot Boy, his mother's favourite son:
  She showed his letters to her friends, then there were none.
Ten little Pilot Boys have gone into obscurity,
  For paying no attention to that vital word Security.
All the little Pilot Boys are wiped clean off the map,
  Because some people will not learn to shut their b----y trap.

and am still fully operational, alive and kicking – in spite of a few unavoidable accidents about which there's no need to go on making those jokes. In any case, I send you my photo to prove I'm me. Publish it if you like for all the clots who don't believe I exist". The letter carried the signature Anthony Armstrong had devised for answering Prune's mail and added a P.S. "And now if anyone says I'm not real you can tell them to pull their finger out". On the opposite page was a 'cod' photograph of Prune

painted by Bill Hooper. This double-page spread would have left the readers of 'Tee Emm' in no doubt that Prune wasn't what he claimed to be; and perhaps it was necessary to put him into a correct perspective for the remainder of his time in the Service.

Prune's character did, however, raise one other problem. If he had spent some years in the RAF it would be virtually impossible to remain at the level

'Prune's' dog 'Binder'.

of Pilot Officer. However, 'Flying Officer Prune' didn't have the same ring and 'Flight Lieutenant Prune' not only sounded ridiculous but went against the basic concept of the meaning of Prune. There was only one solution, a Court Martial; and Anthony Armstrong applied it. In the January 1943 issue of 'Tee Emm', he reported in detail both the prosecution and defence of a charge of 'Making An Unauthorised Flight Contrary To Group Standing Orders'. The crime was insufficient to tarnish Prune's character with 'Tee Emm's' readers (in fact the majority of his exploits were more heinous), who were most likely to be on his side. But, it was nevertheless a technical offence and, although the verdict was never reported, Prune's continued status as a Pilot Officer could have left the readership with few surprises. Such became Prune's fame that he had many imitators; one in particular irritated both Anthony Armstrong and Bill Hooper. It depicted Prune pulling a zip-fastener across his mouth and, in bold lettering, the caption read, 'Take a tip from P.O. Prune: Zip Your Lip!'. Not only was it a colour poster, a luxury not yet afforded to Prune, but the plagiarist appeared to have missed the point – of all people, Prune was famous for being garrulous and, therefore, a security risk. Prune also had his official imitators, or 'cousins' as they were more correctly termed. The first of these came in a Polish version of 'Tee Emm' which merely copied, in a much thickened form, both the humour and the drawings. The Free French Squadrons of the RAF, unable to cope with either the language or the Englishness of the humour, loved the idea of Prune and decided to create their own monthly magazine.

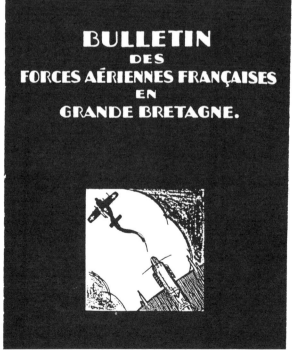

helped them feel less isolated in the structure of the RAF. The magazine was used in a more interpretive role than 'Tee Emm' but, like its mentor, it carried the message far more effectively than bland memoranda written in French. 'Bulletin' suffered from having no official staff and its life was dictated both by the duration of the French Squadrons' period in England and by the ability of Comdt Duperier to sustain the initiative. After he was posted it continued for a short while in other hands but fell by the wayside when the Squadron returned to France, leaving Aspirant la Praline to become a symbol of the time they spent fighting from England's shores.

Commandant B. Duperier FAFL.

'Bulletin des Forces Aeriennes Francaises en Grande Bretagne' was the brainchild of one Commandant Bernard Duperier (together with a Lt. 'Medecin' Berman), who not only knew and understood the content of 'Tee Emm' but had met Bill Hooper briefly when his 'Ile-de-France' Squadron had been temporarily based at Hornchurch in late 1942. Like many Officers, Duperier found himself posted to the Air Ministry in London for a break from the action and he decided to use some of his time there to create the journal they had in mind. First thoughts had been to ask if perhaps Prune could serve in the Free French Air Force as well as the RAF; but it seemed more interesting to suppose that Prune could have a French cousin. Comdt Duperier liked the roundness that Bill Hooper had given to Prune and when he finally asked Hooper to draw the character it was decided to thicken the eyebrows, and capture a French smartness in the very different uniform. Like Prune, he was given the first rank out of Flying School, 'Aspirant', and his name was taken from the childish phrase 'Cul-Cul la Praline' which basically meant idiotic. Aspirant la Praline was a great success with the Free French and 'Bulletin'

l'Aspirant la Praline

Commander A.K. Doyle USN.

incompetent, careless, stupid flier; and his misdeeds were represented in a way that amused pilots - at the same time, or at least that was the theory, they instructed. 'Dilbert', the caption would read, 'always believed in stretching a glide,' and Osborn's cartoon would show a plane, stretched out over a boundary fence like a piece of bubble gum, with Dilbert's complacent lunatic face thrust from the cockpit". In all there were some 2,000 Dilbert posters produced by Osborn, many in colour and in time Dilbert's name entered the vocabulary of Naval pilots and attached itself to every incompetent flier. "Nobody had a name for the brilliant pilots. But the brilliant pilots weren't going to kill you!".

DILBERT

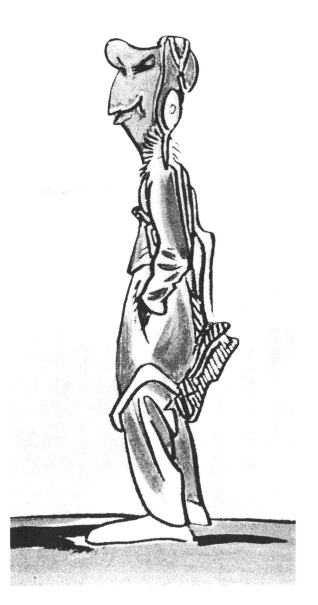

'Dilbert' was quite a different story but the only other major example of a 'duff' pilot used by an Air Force for training during World War Two. Drawn by Robert C. Osborn for the United States Navy Bureau of Aeronautics, he could be seen more as a direct descendant of 'Cloudy Joe' than owing anything to Prune; but even that made them related. Dilbert first appeared in 1942 as the result of a desperate need for the US Navy to reduce the terrible accident rate they were experiencing. "Cadet ranks were suffering considerable losses", Osborn remembers, "They were forgetting to switch fuel tanks, were trying to turn back to the field with engine problems rather than land straight ahead – mistakes of that nature." Commander A.K. Doyle worked with Robert Osborn on the idea of creating a Naval Aviation Cadet who just wouldn't learn. "Whether it is his natural cussedness or sheer stupidity, not even his instructors can say. But, Dilbert loves to show off and this trait makes it possible for cadets to profit from his mistakes". Dilbert appeared only in poster form; but, by 1943, some 300 or so were in circulation. He had been given an accomplice 'Spoiler', the mechanic, and his deaf-dumb-and-blind flying had achieved a marked effect on the flight safety statistics as he taught the cadets "what *not to do* in or with an airplane". Samuel Hynes who trained at the US Marine Corps Air Station at Santa Barbara in 1944 remembered the crew rooms plastered with Dilbert cartoons. "He (Dilbert) was the image of an

Apart from its specific training role, 'Tee Emm's' other big function was to aid the battle against Flying Accidents. Most of these were caused by breaches of the rules, ie: unauthorised low flying, or a sloppy attitude towards Flight Safety - and a campaign was waged on both fronts. Copies of accident reports were handed in to Anthony Armstrong. Each month he would select one which typified the problem at that time by publishing a synopsis of its content under the banner: 'Careless Flying Costs Lives'. The piece was usually quite grim, holding back only on the perpetrator's name; and all carried some form of hard-hitting introduction. "Numbers of civilians have been bumped off, some of them in particularly unpleasant ways. Some have been burnt to death in their homes; at least one unfortunate has been literally carved in two by a prop. as he was working peacefully on his farm. We know of parents who have watched their sons go up in flames and smoke on the front doorstep, and of girl-friends who have seen a lump of charred flesh instead of the good-looking chap they had hoped to marry". Most of these items showed a photograph of the result of

the incident and served as an awful warning of what could happen if the regulations were flouted. As deliberately anti-humour as this approach was, humour was also used in the campaign and Bill Hooper produced several drawings based on lesser incidents setting out to portray the perpetrators as 'Dim', 'Bad Mannered' or just 'Rather Poor Pilots'. Prune was also used but the nature of his character prevented him from ever being displayed as deliberately breaking the rules – his accidents were usually trangressions caused by a lack of adequate thinking.

'Tee Emm's' effort, which was only a part of the total campaign against accidents, appeared to be successful but, in December 1943, the Permanent Under-Secretary of State for Air, Sir Arthur Street, addressed himself to the problem. In a memorandum circulated to all Air Officers Commanding in Home Commands, he wrote that there was a continuing decrease in the number of accidents, "but the greater number of hours flown (per accident) and cost and complexity of modern aircraft and larger crews carried have more than offset such saving in

The Awful Tale of P.O. Prune

Who could not concentrate,
Adapted from a Station Mag.
And used to Illustrate
A Moral Suitable for Those
Who would avoid Prune's Fate

This is the tale of P.O Prune,
Now in hospital at Frome,
Who, though Industrious and Keen,

The type who keeps his buttons clean,
Earned for himself a bitter fate,
Because he could not concentrate.

human lives or material as would otherwise have resulted. Accordingly, it is of vital importance to the air effort that the present serious losses caused by Flying Accidents should be further substantially reduced". He ended by announcing the formation of a Directorate of Accident Prevention in the AMT's Office to be headed up by the then Deputy Director of Operational Training, Group Captain H.D. O'Neill. The existence of this new Directorate only served to increase the impetus and Anthony Armstrong was briefed to apply even stronger emphasis to the problem in 'Tee Emm'. A sloppy

attitude towards Flight Safety was another matter. And because that fitted with the demeanour of Prune, it was easy to use him to ram home the importance of such things as 'Pilot's Notes', 'Cockpit Drill' or 'Form 700'. This was a form designed to be filled in by all returning Pilots if they had experienced any fault whatsoever with the aircraft during flight. Being yet another piece of paper, exhausted Pilots returning from a sortie tended, unless the fault was obviously serious, to treat this as another piece of 'Bumph' and merely told the Duty Officer or one of the groundcrew.

Although he always tried his best
To be Efficient (like the rest),
He simply hadn't got the skill
To concentrate on COCKPIT
    DRILL.

He tried mnemonics ; used to sit
For ages memorising it.
But once inside his aeroplane,
He just forgot it all again.

The inter-com., the airscrew pitch,
The warning indicator switch,
The flaps, and elevator trim,
Were one and all alike to him.

He happened then in course of time
To muddle up this pantomime,
Whilst coming in to land one day
In (what he thought) the usual way.

He accidentally pulled the catch,
That jettisons the exit hatch.
It quite surprised him when he saw
His gunner vanish through the floor,
Then hurtle downwards through
    the air,—
To burst beside the signal square.

Poor P.O Prune in pensive mood,
Forgot to check his altitood,
And at a hundred miles per hour
He cannoned off the water tower,
Mowed down an Orderly Parade,
Then hit the deck and ricochetted
Right through the Mess, wherein a
    bunch
Of Officers were taking lunch.

Imagine then the screams and
    groans,
The crunching sound of splintered
    bones,
The shattered glass, the ruptured
    seams,
The tangled mass of twisted beams,
The *débris* scattered everywhere.
It was a Terrible Affair.

When all was clear they took the
    dead
And heaped them in the tractor
    shed,
They counted them and found at
    length
That fully half the ration strength
Were incapacitated, or
Revolting messes on the floor.

From 'midst the havoc he had
    wrought
They dug Prune from his Jugger-
    naut.
The doctor hastily arrived—
And found, alas, he had *survived*.

Next day Group Captain Chol-
    mondly-Pym
Severely reprimanded him ;
A punishment both wise and just,
For pilots in the Service must
(Lest they should share P.O Prune's
    fate)
Be capable
    and CONCENTRATE.

But just like the Pilots, Duty Officers and groundcrew changed roster and, often with more important things to worry about, verbal information, on what at first might look like an insignificant fault, did not always get passed on. The result of this was that, on occasions, 'unserviceable' aircraft were unwittingly sent into action, sometimes with the loss of both aircraft and crew. Engineers and test Pilots, unaware of the exact nature of the fault, could also find themselves in critical danger and more than one maintenance crew found itself becoming an unfortunate and costly mess on the runway during take-off. There were far too many of these incidents logged by Investigating Officers in their Accident Reports and, in addition to the potential loss of life, it was costly in both manhours and flying time.

Reminders to fill in 'Form 700' correctly cropped up in almost every issue of 'Tee Emm', and it wasn't until after the war, when the pressure was off, that the situation began to ease. The problem of unauthorised low flying continued to plague the Air Ministry, reasserting itself again in 1946.

By the end of 1941, 'Tee Emm' had settled down to a print run of 21,000 copies per month distributed throughout the RAF and printed by a single printer in England. Copies were also supplied to the Admiralty for distribution to the Fleet Air Arm and also to the War Office for use in certain training establishments. As the Service continued to expand demands began to build for an increased allocation of copies to Canada, Australia, South Africa and various other places where the RAF was congregating. Also the US Army 8th Air Force, operational in Britain from August 1942, requested to be included on the circulation list. Faced by difficulties with transportation out of Britain and a shortage of paper supply, it was obvious that alternative arrangements had to be made, and in 1943, some reorganisation made it possible for copies to be printed overseas as well. In all, 'Tee Emm' was printed in seven different centres – including Washington DC in the USA – covering all five continents; print orders varying from place to place according to local requirement. It is estimated that at its peak it reached a circulation of over 30,000 copies a month, making both 'Tee Emm' and 'Pilot Officer Prune' household names throughout the Allied Air Forces. With such a large and worldwide coverage (readership would have been probably double the circulation figure) it is no wonder that news of Prune crept out past the 'Official Use Only' net. Originally 'Tee Emm' had contained some technical and tactical material which had to be cleared by one of the Air Intelligence departments but two years into its life, the emphasis began to change. 'Tee Emm', while manifestly the same, started to act more as a reminder, or pointer, and its content was significantly more anecdotal, containing little or none of the specific tactical or

Staff Artist W. Hooper and WAFF Section Officer 'Copper' in 'Tee Emm's' Office 1946.

technical information originally published. It had by that time acquired an almost anarchic quality of its own; and, as was subsequently proven, its ideas and style were virtually unstoppable. It had a regular monthly readership which could hardly wait to see what Anthony Armstrong was going to write or to learn the latest blunders of Pilot Officer Prune.

Anthony Armstrong and Bill Hooper worked well together according to Mrs Monica Willis, Armstrong's wife. They had a sense of humour that was different but complementary and were able to spark one another into humorous ideas which could wander off on tangents. Because of this, or perhaps in spite of it, they decided to reveal Prune, and their view of the RAF, to the public at large in a series of pocket-size books. Anthony Armstrong, with an already long list of successful books behind him, was well-established with several publishers and knew exactly what the market required. So he set about structuring a basic format they could follow. Since Anthony Armstrong was the acknowledged

pen name of Flight Lieutenant (soon to be Squadron Leader) A.A. Willis, he had no problem in using it but Aircraftman W.J. Hooper, obliged under Service Regulations to adopt a pseudonym for anything he did privately, chose to call himself 'Raff'. The first book in the series was 'Plonk's Party' in which Prune was only revealed towards the end. In their second production, 'Prune's Progress', Anthony Armstrong strove to build up the family background of the fictional Pilot Officer. 'Nice Types' came next, to be followed in turn by 'More Nice Types' and 'Goodbye Nice Types'. Anthony Armstrong ended the series with a book on his own, 'Prangmere Mess', which comprised a collection of the Prune stories he had published in 'Punch' during the preceding years. Printed on 'War Economy Standard' paper but with coloured dust jackets these little books were considered a huge success, some running into several editions. They brought to the public a brief insight into how the 'Boys in Blue' laughed at themselves and revealed something of the nature of the Royal Air Force's worst kept secret.

"A book for Official Use Only
Must not mention authors by name
Thus nobody gets any credit
But nobody gets any blame!"

(Tee Emm - 1942)

FIGHTER COMMAND

Pilot Officer Prune was essentially a product of Fighter Command and more particularly of No. 11 Group, because that was where Bill Hooper had spent most of his active service, and it remained the main source of visual reference. Like most of the 'Heroes' who captured the headlines, Prune was a 'Glory Boy', as the Press dubbed both the Spitfire and Hurricane Pilots shortly after the Battle of Britain. Of the two aircraft Prune was nearly always depicted flying a Spitfire which, due to the beauty of its elliptical wings and its edge on performance over the Hurricane, had the romantic image of a sports car of the skies. In fact, although the Spitfire was tasked to operate at higher altitude and was used to attack the fighters that gave high cover to the enemy bombers - it was the Hurricane that dominated the Battle of Britain. During the three and a half months of the action, there were about three Hurricane Squadrons to every two of Spitfires (this remained constant throughout the Battle of Britain because Hurricanes were quicker to build and their metal frame and fabric construction was less affected by enemy guns). However, by the time 'Tee Emm' first appeared the balance had changed with Spitfire production (due to shadow factories coming on line) steadily catching up. Night Fighters were also beginning to play a significant role in defence with Squadrons of Defiants and Blenheims in the early days of the Blitz. And, it became important for Prune not to be seen as just a 'Glory Boy' but to fly all of the different aircraft of Fighter Command, even if, occasionally, he wasn't quite certain which one was which. This point was well made by 'Tee Emm', which like Prune, was prone to the 'odd' mistake. The Beaufort, seen making a one-wheel landing underneath Prune, in the title drawing opposite, was actually used to illustrate a piece by Anthony Armstrong on an emergency landing made by a shot-up Beaufighter.

True to his origins, of which Anthony Armstrong thoroughly approved, Prune was always a Fighter Pilot at heart. Despite the fact that, because of the demands of 'Tee Emm', he had to be in all Commands for all people, nevertheless he retained the characteristics that were particular to a Fighter 'type'. In many respects this made sense for he was an individual, one of a kind, and hopefully the only one as far as the Royal Air Force was concerned. Fighter Pilots were all highly individual both in their dress and their manner and therefore Prune was easily accepted as being a particularly dimwitted version of one of them. Prune sported all their trademarks and apart from the ubiquitous scarf

(used to cover up the lack of an Officer's regulation stiff collar and tie – almost impossible to wear while flying) he was invariably depicted with the top button of his 'Best Blue' tunic left undone. This was a popular affectation among Fighter Pilots which was sometimes carried to extremes. There are several photographs showing Squadrons on parade receiving decorations from His Majesty King George VI where a large proportion of the Pilots had left their top buttons open. The origin of this habit is unclear and claims have been made that it enabled a Pilot to button his R/T cord out of the way or that it prevented discomfort when strapped into a tight cockpit by a Sutton Harness. But, it is more likely that it was a deliberate attempt to be different and to separate the Fighters from the so-called 'Bus Drivers' of Bomber Command. Prune's other principal trademark, apart from his inordinate scruffiness which wasn't exactly unheard of among Fighter Command Pilots in the early 1940s, was the large patched tear in his service cap. Fighter Pilots who preferred to wear a dress cap, as opposed to the 'field service' side cap, had a problem if it was necessary to carry it in the cockpit. This was sometimes the case because if a 'chap' was intending to land out at another RAF Station he would be improperly dressed without a cap once he had left his aircraft. To facilitate the

Strategy and tactics while awaiting the call to 'Scramble'.

dress cap's travel in the cockpit Fighter Pilots would remove the buckram stiffener, or have their cap made without, so that becoming soft and pliable it would tuck-in easily somewhere safe during flight. Logically Prune would get his entangled with some sharp piece of metal and, short of funds for a replacement, would ineptly repair the resultant gash. (Prune thought his 'Batman' had something to do with marshalling aircraft). Thus Prune's patched dress cap as well as his polka-dot scarf became the lasting symbols of his Fighter Pilot origins, no matter where he was posted through the pages of 'Tee Emm'.

A Fighter Squadron usually comprised twelve aircraft and twenty-four Pilots, divided into two Flights, 'A' and 'B'. A normal Duty Roster would provide for one Flight to be at 'Readiness' while the other was stood down. But, since action took place at any time from first to last light, summer could mean a 4 am start for the first Flight on Duty. No single Flight ever consistently mustered its full complement of twelve Pilots because there would be losses, those that were medically unfit or the lucky ones who had managed to obtain a 48-hour leave pass. On average nine to ten Pilots would be available for the six aircraft; and, at times when a 'Panic' was on and both Flights were

from its prime defensive role and with co-ordinated daylight sorties of 'Rhubarbs' (general 'Fighter Sweeps') and 'Circuses' (mixed bomber and fighter raids) rapidly changed from the

RAFF.

being held at 'Readiness' together, it could become vital to get every possible aircraft into the air. This was very often the case during the Battle of Britain, the spare Pilots being given aircraft that were undergoing minor servicing in order to form a third Flight. By 1941, Fighter Command had turned

'Scramble' image of the Battle of Britain more towards the 'offensive'. That is not to say 'Panics' and 'Duffs' didn't continue but more usually operations would be based on a clear briefing, backed by Photographic Reconnaissance, with a defined target - even if it was just to call up the Luftwaffe and draw them into air battle.

Service Terms Illustrated
by
Well-known Newspaper Cartoonists
No. 2. ILLINGWORTH of the Daily Mail.

CIRCUITS AND BUMPS

Squadron Leader A.A. Willis as depicted by his friend 'Illingworth' in 'Tee Emm'.

PLATE 1.

P.O. Prune's definition of a good landing is one you can walk away from.

W. HOOPER
R.A.F.

231

This page from 'Tee Emm' was coloured by a Pilot's girlfriend as a 'Good Luck Charm'
for him to carry while he was flying. Apparently it worked since he survived the
War in Bomber Command despite the clear breach of the OUO rules.

PLATE 2.

The normal routine was for a Pilot to check and prepare his designated aircraft the moment he came on duty. Together with the Groundcrew he would run up the engine, complete a full preflight check, both exterior and interior, and then leave his helmet, gloves, etc., together with his parachute and harness straps laid out in 'Readiness' according to the manner that suited him. The aircraft were usually positioned in the 'revetments' or scattered around the Dispersal Point, always facing the direction of take-off and, where necessary, with a Trolley Accumulator already attached. The Flights, under their respective Flight Commanders, were designated into Sections: 'A' Flight comprising Red, Yellow and White and 'B' Flight made up of Blue, Green and Black. The ideal take-off was always made in 'V' Formation whether it was by Flight or the whole Squadron; and 'dispersed' aircraft were usually parked with a predetermined Section order in mind.

'Scramble', the code for immediate take-off at the approach of enemy aircraft, was the operative word at which the Pilots in their Flight Hut would jump to their feet. Money, cards or whatever would fly into the air and they would dive for the door. Already wearing their 'Mae West' lifejackets they would run to their aircraft and leap into the cockpit to be helped into their straps by an attendant member of the Groundcrew.

LINES FROM PRUNE'S SHOOTING GALLERY

I leave my top button undone because I haven't got one: it was shot off in a dog fight.

A 'Flight' of Spitfires breaks into the attack.

If the enemy was close, seconds were critical and the moment a Pilot was ready he would give a 'thumbs-up' to the 'bod' on the starter trolley and fire up his engine. In this situation there was no etiquette for take-off, it was important just to get airborne and the correct formation would be formed during the climb to operational altitude. The call to 'Scramble' would always be accompanied by a preliminary instruction (ie. " 'A' Flight Scramble, Bandits Maidstone, Angels-Two-Five"). But, once

airborne the Flight Commander would be controlled by 'Operations' via the R/T and instructions would invariably be modified. Although it took only a few minutes to get the Flight or Squadron into the air it would take a minimum of some ten or twelve minutes to be in the required position at operational height and even longer if those 'Scrambled' were ordered to form up with other Squadrons. 'Scramble' was the keyword of the Battle of Britain when squadrons would be at 'Readiness' seven days of the week and stand downs might only last as long as it took to get something to eat in the Mess. During that period aircraft would return from a sortie only to be refuelled, rearmed and sent straight back up into the fight with a turn around of some twenty-five to thirty-five minutes – and that several times a day. Many a Pilot found himself being thrust skyward and into the fray when only few minutes earlier the combined effects of stress and sheer exhaustion had almost overcome him.

Backed by Winston Churchill's famous 'The Few' speech it was this form of 'Scramble' existence with its dogfights visible in the skies over Southern England that, aided by Fleet Street and the BBC broadcasts, formed the lasting image and created the mythology of Fighter Command. But, by 1941, 'Scrambles' were few and far between with a new form of tension entering the Fighter Pilots' experience. And, 'chaps' briefed for a 'Rhubarb' or a

COLLECTION HANS OERKE

German propaganda photograph (faked).

'Circus' (and later a 'Rodeo') could find themselves at 'Readiness' for several hours with their aircraft dispersed across the airfield in take-off formation, awaiting an improved 'Met situation' or a reconnaissance update before a green 'Very' flare would signal the 'off'. Instead of a brief flight up into the battle they faced an hour or more of flying before they confronted the enemy.

Absolute 'norms' did not exist in Fighter Command, it was a flexible force by the very nature of its being. Many variations existed between Squadrons, both in their organisation and their approach to battle tactics. Once airborne, the Flights or Squadrons would be in direct contact with the Operations Room at their Sector Station which in turn were in constant contact with Fighter Command Group Headquarters – and were receiving constant updates from 'RDF' Station Plotters ('Radar' as it was eventually to be called), the Royal Observer Corps and other airborne Squadrons under their control. R/T chatter was kept to a minimum between Pilots in the air to keep the airwaves clear. Operations would issue its instructions in a simple and continually revised code so that a listening enemy was unable to interpret immediately the tactical pattern. The Operations Room was under the charge of the Controller who, together with the Intelligence Officer, formed the backbone of a Squadron in Fighter Command. The Controller strictly belonged to the Sector 'Ops'

Room and would be in charge of the activities of several Squadrons. It was his responsibility to think and plan ahead on the plotting table by implementing Group's instructions to a practical effect set against the latest information. A good Controller would ensure that the Flights or Squadrons under him were suitably positioned to enter a confrontation with the enemy to their best advantage. But, once the enemy had been engaged they broke from his control and either fought as a team

W. HOOPER
R.A.F.

or individually, dependent on both the nature of the operation and the Squadron's own tactical approach. The Controller had always been a Pilot himself, was usually an older man and was kept well briefed on both policy and warfare tactics by Group Headquarters. Good Controllers were creative inasmuch as they ran their side of an operation on instinct, knowing when to trust or to distrust incoming reports. Flight Commanders grew to have their favourites and knew that, with the right man at the end of the radio, they would make visual contact with the enemy long before he could see them.

Good Control also created a problem in Fighter Command which Prune was quick to latch onto – if Control knew exactly how to get you there, then it would know exactly how to get you home. This lazy approach to navigation wasn't much of a problem during the Battle of Britain when engagements and patrols would be within short range of the home airfield. Pilots would, in any event, get to know the various landmarks of their 'patch'. But, with the advent of 'Fighter Sweeps' where individual chases could soon split up a Squadron on the other side of the Channel, attention to navigation became of prime importance – especially since R/T chatter to Control would merely give away to the enemy an accurate position and intention. 'Tee

Emm' hammered the point in 1941, first in June: "We are staggered. People seem actually to be coming round to the idea that navigation matters. Even our P.O. Prune has admitted this – after having been heard to express surprised pleasure at finding that the Scharnhorst and Gneisenau had at last been sunk – and then discovering he was over Lorient, not Brest". In October of that year, Anthony Armstrong addressed the problem again in a long article, with a tone of admonishment, entitled 'Are Fighters Paupers'. In it he referred to the: "bad habits of Fighters many of whom think the compass is there to scrape the clay off their boots when entering the cockpit". It was a double-edged sword, "you can't easily teach old Fighter Aces (well, over 21, that is) new tricks", and it was important not to discourage the use of Control to guide home a battle-damaged aircraft. The problem mainly stemmed from vanity (a fresh crop of Pilots who wanted to emulate their Battle of Britain heroes) and from the first batches of Pilots coming on line from the Empire Air Training Scheme, where map reading had often meant following a railway track across miles of featureless and empty landscape. It was a problem that only arose during the transition of Fighter Command from a defensive to an offensive role, since all subsequent intakes at the Operational Training Units were prepared adequately for their revised requirement as Pilots.

THE HUN IS NOT DEAF.

I SAY! YOU CHAPS ARE THEY OUR'S OR THEIR'S?
AH! THE BLENHEINS ARE HERE! GOOD SHOW THAT MAKES TWO
SQUADRONS OF BOMBERS....DUM DUM ANNIE LOURIE THATS
FUNNY I THOUGHT WE WERE ONLY 3 SQUADRONS OF FIGHTERS
WELL HERE WE ARE BLOKES. LOOK AT THAT FLAK!

W.HOOPER R.A.F.

Radio Telephony (R/T) discipline in general was another problem with replacement Pilots fresh from OTUs that plagued Fighter Command. It was one thing to establish good practice during training but, faced with the real enemy, or separated from the rest of the Squadron, there was a tendency for a 'new boy' to get either over-excited in the heat of battle or a 'bit panicky' at finding himself alone and to clutter up the airwaves with unnecessary verbiage or let slip a snippet of vital information. The Germans had a series of receiving stations situated along the French, Belgian and Dutch coasts. These maintained a 24-hour watch and were operated by girls who had worked abroad and were fluent in all of the Allied languages. The receivers could reach well into South Eastern England covering all VHF frequencies. Information gleaned was then logged, together with a D/F (Direction Finder) fix on the source of the signal, and passed immediately to Intelligence at the various Luftwaffe bases. Prune, who in the early days had seen the R/T as a useful device for ordering bacon and eggs from the Mess to be ready on his return, frowned on its frivolous use and was prone to repeating important tactical information over the airwaves in order to provide a running commentary for those who may have been asleep at the briefing. Unlike the Pilots, the Controller back in his Operations Room, at least had the choice of whether or not to listen.

Skill plus luck brought this battle damaged Spitfire home.

'Spy', the Intelligence Officer, debriefs returning Pilots.

The Intelligence Officer was altogether a different animal from the Controller. 'Spy', as he was known in most Fighter Squadrons, was often thought of as a ponderous intellectual 'type' – 'Wingless' and often rushing around on a bicycle with a notebook trying to obtain the required information. In practice he was also an older man and commanded some respect – there were young Intelligence Officers but they tended to be teased mercilessly by the Pilots. His job was vital and the reports of action that he collected from each Pilot after an action would build up a picture that could in turn be analysed at Group Headquarters. It was these Intelligence Reports that were used by Fighter Command for Forward Planning and lessons learnt could also result in a modification of Strategy and Air Tactics. It was also his task to 'log' and verify the 'kill' claims made by individual Pilots and it was there that contention started. If a Pilot shot down an enemy aircraft, saw pieces fly off and saw it either spin out-of-control or dive in smoke towards the ground, he might be entitled to believe he had shot it down. But, in a sky full of swooping, diving, twisting aircraft, all seemingly firing at one another, it was unwise to follow the victim and ensure its fate. Likewise more that one Pilot would fire at the same aircraft and by time the report reached the Intelligence Officer it would be counted twice or even three times.

"Ensure your rudder pedals are correctly adjusted."

TEN LITTLE FIGHTER BOYS

Ten Little Fighter boys taking off in Line
One was in coarse pitch, then there were nine
Nine little fighter boys climbing "through the gate"
One's petrol wasn't on, then there were eight
Eight little fighter boys scrambling up to heaven
One weaver didn't and then there were seven
Seven little fighter boys up to all the tricks
One had a hangover then there were six
Six little fighter boys milling over Hythe
One's pressure wasn't up and then there were five
Five little fighter boys over France's shore
One flew reciprocal and then there were four
Four little fighter boys joining in the spree
One's sight wasn't on and then there were three
Three little fighter boys high up in the blue
One's rubber pipe was loose then there were two
Two little fighter boys homing out of sun
Flew straight and level and then there was one
One little fighter boy happy to be home
Beat up dispersal and then there were none
Ten little Spitfires nothing have achieved
A.O.C at Group is very very peeved
"Fifty thousand Smackers thrown down the drains
'Cause Ten Silly baskets didn't use their brains"

WHOOPER

The Air Ministry laid down rules defining enemy casualties:

'Destroyed' – Aircraft must be seen on the ground or in the air destroyed by a member of the crew or formation, or confirmed from other sources, eg. ships at sea, local authorities, etc. – Aircraft must be seen to descend with flames issuing. It is not sufficient if only smoke is seen. – Aircraft must be seen to break-up in the air.

'Probables' – When the Pilot of a single-engine aircraft is seen to bale out. – The aircraft was seen to break off the combat in circumstances which would lead our Pilots to believe it will be a loss. A further category was 'Damaged' but as far as kills were concerned this didn't count towards the total or 'Tally'.

Shared 'kills' were listed as fractions and it took five fully confirmed destroyed aircraft before a Fighter Pilot could be termed, albeit unofficially, an 'Ace'. Sorting all this out was a nightmare for the Intelligence Officer, who had to make repeated requests to outside authorities, including the Army and the Navy, to confirm reports he had managed to unscramble. Added to which, the Intelligence Officer was often the last person a Pilot wanted to see when he had just landed back 'on a wing and a prayer' after a particularly harrowing sortie. Prune

to be a good Pilot, since the 'weaving' and 'dicing' involved in positioning an aircraft to best advantage in combat was vital – it was also vital to be able to shoot accurately. Poor results in accuracy gave rise to the idea that perhaps the heavy emphasis on Pilot Training was producing the wrong attitude to the Fighter Pilot's role. "The Fighter Pilot's training has been largely designed to produce a Pilot and he is naturally inclined to look upon a Fighter aircraft more as a flying machine. That is all wrong. A Fighter aircraft is really a gun platform

Groundcrew hastily rearming a Hurricane between sorties.

was depicted by Bill Hooper delivering his version of the combat with well gesticulated details of exactly how it happened. Of Prune it was later said that the Intelligence Officer was probably the only person prepared to listen to his stories. To which some wit added "there are Intelligence Officers and Intelligent Officers!".

Marksmanship, which was the 'stuff' of which 'Aces' were made, was a theme constantly addressed by 'Tee Emm'. Whereas it was important

and nothing more. It is not intended as a sort of aerial super-sports car in which it is fun to hare around the skies. It is meant as a fighting machine which must be pointed in the right direction, as not as a means of joy-riding. So first you learn to fly; then you must learn to shoot while flying". The eight .303 Browning machine-guns fitted to both the Spitfire and the Hurricane fired at a rate of 11-1200 rounds per minute, all of the guns fired together and the ammunition belt for each gun only contained between 320 and 350 rounds. Therefore,

W. HOOPER.
R.A.F.

the Fighter Pilot had just 16 or so seconds of fire power when he entered combat and he needed to use it sparingly – a single burst or 'squirt' not exceeding one second unless he could be absolutely certain of his target. Reflector sights were used to improve deflection shooting (the speed of the target times the speed of the bullet related to the angle between them). In the fray of battle with varying closing speeds it wasn't easy to get it right. Good marksmen were often instinctive but it could be taught by continual practise with the deflector sight. "Close Range and Accurate Sighting" were the words stated and restated with 'Close' being given to mean almost aerial contact, which was in effect 200 yards or less. In the excitement of a engagement it was not easy to estimate how much ammunition had been expended but by late 1940 cine-guns were being added to Fighter aircraft, to aid Intelligence analysis, these had a footage counter which read in the cockpit and gave the Pilot a rough idea.

Twenty-millimetre cannon were gradually fitted to fighter aircraft dependent on their role but these merely demanded better marksmanship for instead of the spread from eight guns there was just two twin lines of fire, albeit that the results on impact were considerably more devastating. Nervous Pilots tended either to give 'too many' bursts or 'too long' a burst at an unsure target, running out of ammunition early and becoming a danger to the

Squadron because they would then have to rely on others to protect them. This bad habit had to be stamped out and 'Tee Emm' pushed for 'bags' of practise in marksmanship. Even Prune admitted to: "an acute sense of embarrassment on being mixed up with a bunch of 109s with no ammunition in his guns".

One less to worry about (Do 17).

W.HOOPER.

" I can't see a word you're saying."

Night Fighters, although part of Fighter Command, were a different breed. Their role was to attack and pick-off incoming enemy night raiders. Later in the war this was extended to accompanying Bomber Command raids and attacking the defending German night fighters. In 1940 the early

Night Fighting Squadrons were composed of Hurricanes and Defiants who went up to look around, vectored into position by Control. But, by the end of the year AI (Air Interception - an aspect of 'RDF/Radar') was beginning to become available and the new generation of Night Fighters composed a team of Pilot and AI Operator, usually an Air Gunner, flying specially converted twin-engine Beaufighters and Mosquitos. Vectored onto a 'Bandit' the AI Operator would locate the enemy as a blip on his cathode-ray tube and would control the aircraft by instructions to the Pilot on both position and speed. Unlike the ordinary Fighter Pilot, who hunted in packs, the Night Fighter was a solo operator and used tracking and stealth to locate and score a 'kill'. Quality of night vision was critical for the Pilots who could find themselves suddenly on top of the enemy and to preserve this they wore dark glasses during daylight periods before flying. This, as well as a different sort of personality, separated them from the normal Fighter Pilots. Night Flying training was done in the daylight with the Pilot wearing suitably darkened goggles. Prune, liking the idea of being able to fly without anyone seeing his mistakes, put in for a training course. Fortunately he never quite grasped the idea.

Crew climb abroad a Blenheim Night Fighter.

Is Your Accident Really Necessary

Flight Safety reminders remained a priority throughout 'Tee Emm' and special attention was paid to the Fighter Command problem of unauthorised low flying and the 'beating up' of girlfriends' or family houses.

A frequent image was of 'Prune' Pilot, wearing an alternative set of wings, in deep conversation with one of St Peter's Angels or an ethereal RAF Officer who had made the same mistake.

Accident Prevention was an important aspect of 'Tee Emm's' role.

IT MAKES YOU THINK ! ! !

HARK to the story of Christopher Spink,
    A young Sergeant Pilot (from Sydney, we think),
Who never from danger nor hazard did shrink,
But suffered from one most unfortunate kink—
He just wouldn't practise I.F. in the Link.

One day, while returning to base o'er the drink,
The weather clamped down with a sky black as ink
And twenty-tenths cloud showing never a chink.
What happened that day caused a terrible stink ;
For Christopher's flying just went on the blink,
And the capers he cut would make anyone think
That he'd rammed in his finger right up to the brink.

To cut short our story and save H.M.'s ink,
Our unhappy Chris finished up in the drink.
The kite was a write-off, and as you might think,
The poor duty pilot, in fear that he'd sink,
Until he was rescued, slept never a wink.

At the Court of Enquiry the Acting Chief Gink
Examined C.'s Log Book for times in the Link.
When he found sweet F.A. he raised such a stink
That C. was court-martialled and landed in clink
With practically nothing to do there but think.

But he thought to some purpose, and ironed out his kink,
And now Flying Officer Christopher Spink,
(D.F.C. and two bars), a most popular gink,
Makes a habit of standing sprog pilots a drink.
And to aid their refreshment he tips them the wink
That the way to keep out of the drink and the clink
Is by taking small regular doses of Link.

W. HOOPER

Tactics were a very important part of Fighter Command training and would frequently be changed or modified with the introduction of new techniques to counteract those implemented by the enemy. Fighting Tactics were laid down in the publication of 'Tactical Instructions' by the Command in 'Air Ministry Tactical Papers'. One of these, 'Fighting Talk', which was illustrated by David Langdon, followed the style of 'Tee Emm' and although Prune never put in an appearance the concept was the same. 'Tee Emm', because of its OUO classification (Official Use Only) and its very large circulation, was considered to be at too low a security level for such important information and Prune's task was merely to refer to the existence of 'Fighting Talk' as a reminder to seek out a copy and study it. The closest 'Tee Emm' could get to Tactics was to reinforce the values of the

" The North Wind doth blow, And we shall have snow,
And what will poor Spitfire do then, poor thing ?
Completely earth-bound, She'll sit on the ground,
Till somebody's Snow-plan gets cracking, poor thing !"
Traditional (or very nearly).

various techniques employed for learning. One of these was the 'Link Trainer', one of the first 'real' flight simulators. Built like a 'toy' aircraft but large enough for the trainee to sit inside with an enclosing 'blind' canopy, it had full axes movements with operational flying controls and recorded its track onto a plotting table manned by a 'Link' Supervisor. Fundamentally its purpose was for Instrument Flying practise in Pilot Training and Prune delighted in demonstrating its further possibilities. A variant of this developed for Fighter Command was the 'Fisher' trainer. This was a 'Link' in which a Pilot could sit and 'chase' a model enemy aircraft travelling around the room. "A nice toy this; you fire the gun which shoots a light, which hits the target; and then rings a bell. Or doesn't". The aim was to teach 'deflection shooting' and was part of the 'PGITW' course at the Central Gunnery School. Anthony Armstrong suggested these strange collection of initials might stand for "Prunes, Get Into The War!". In fact it was correctly 'Pilot Gunnery Instructors' Training Wing' – a name which was later changed to simply the Fighter Wing at the Central Gunnery School. Apart from publication of the more obvious Training and Flight Safety

material, 'Tee Emm' was used to get ideas moving or to reinforce an issue that had already been passed down from Fighter Command Headquarters to the Squadrons.

Orders were orders but sometimes, as with the 'Snow Plan' of 1943 (see above), which was about suitable preparation in anticipation of bad weather, action rested on the personal initiative of individual Officers and Senior NCOs. In some ways this was an area in which Prune was at his most effective since he could make direct criticism by demonstrating the pitfalls of 'failing to take suitable action'. Fighter Pilots, because of their highly individualistic nature and their given identity of 'Knights of the Air', were prone to finding themselves a little aloof from some of the basic 'discipline' that was needed to keep a Fighter Squadron on its toes. Pilot Officer Prune was primed to epitomise that attitude. Since no-one wished to assume his identity, although many unwittingly found themselves dubbed as Prunes, the humour of the Anti-Hero worked and a simple dose of Prune applied to problem area usually sorted it out.

" Absolutely nothing to 'em, old boy —"

Humour, both black and white, was the prime antidote to stress and fear - and Fighter Command, possibly because of the Battle of Britain and the high profile its Pilots received, became the principal source for a brand of humour that was to become legion throughout the RAF. Jokes abounded

between members of the groundcrews and although an aircraft's crew could find themselves so attached to its Pilot that they would shed tears if they knew he wasn't going to return from a sortie, their jokes rarely transgressed a mythical line. Likewise the Pilots, almost like an exclusive club, developed a kind of sophisticated sixth-form Public School humour which was held as their preserve and included the art of the laconic response. This particular form of verbal shorthand was rooted in the British tendency for understatement and gave rise to many of the slang expressions of the RAF. 'Stationmaster' for the Commanding Officer of the Aerodrome; 'Fan' for the aircraft's propeller; 'A Good Show' for some exemplary deed of courage; and 'A Piece of Cake' for some masterly achievement (see below opposite for Prune's understanding of its meaning). Immodesty about flying prowess and combat action was strictly frowned on and in these particular instances the qualitative value of understatement was taken to ridiculous extremes. The more excessive the understatement, the more meritorious the action or valour that had probably been involved. Those who said anything which could have been either a gross exaggeration or

"There I was upside down with nothing on the clock but the maker's name."

merely a statement of fact about something which ought not to have been mentioned, were relegated to the 'Line Shooters Club'. 'Tee Emm' published some of the best ones in its 'Lines from Prune's Shooting Gallery' which included such classics as "I never pull the stick back when I'm flying low, in case my tail wheel hits the ground." (see also pages 35 and 50). Many 'Line Shoots' were apocryphal and many were attributed, quite justifiably, to Prune. In the Officers' Mess at Fighter Stations a book was kept for 'Line Shoots' and the evidence of two independent Officers was required before an entry could be made, naming names, to go on permanent display for all to see. Entries were made regardless of rank and one visiting Wing Commander who was told about the existence of the book laughed and stated: "I never shoot lines." His remark, suitably witnessed, was immediately entered into the book. Another entry, referring to a 'near miss' report concerning two landing aircraft, read: "There was at least the width of two visiting cards between us". Thus there was understatement and understated understatement which would be considered overstatement and therefore a 'Line Shoot'. Prune was destined, via Anthony Arm-

"Made in Germany, finished in England."

strong, to become a past master of this particular humour and was directly responsible for such evergreens as "A good landing is one you can walk away from!" (see colour plate page 34).

Prune's version of 'A Piece of Cake'!

LINES FROM PRUNE'S SHOOTING GALLERY

I'm not guilty of bad flying. Landing with one's undercart up is just a mistake.

Although the humour of Prune was consciously created, his mannerisms were derivative and he seemed at times to extend beyond the talents of both Anthony Armstrong and Bill Hooper by stealing control of his own destiny. It may have been that Prune, by his very existence, caused incidents to come to light that otherwise would have been lost in some dusty file. Or, it may have been that Prune's style began to influence the Pilots, as was rumoured to be feared by at least one Member of Air Staff. As the War progressed the real world and the fiction of Prune sometimes seemed to merge. A combat report published in 'Tee Emm' demonstrates the point.

"When close to the French Coast, Blue Section were detailed to investigate an aircraft flying west to east at 300 feet. Blue 1 made a port quarter attack, diving on the aircraft which made a steep turn to port. From the plan view, Blue 1 identified it as a Ju.88 and fired one burst ahead of the aircraft. As the aircraft straightened out, Blue 1 saw roundels, and on following it down to sea level and approaching very close, identified it this time as a Beaufighter with day camouflage. No lettering was visible to our Pilot. Blue 2 followed in and gave two bursts which fell short and was unsure of the identity of the aircraft. The aircraft made off at high speed in a northerly direction".

Anthony Armstrong commented: "And no wonder - after having been mistaken for a Hun. On the other hand the Beaufighter's identification didn't seem so hot either since on his return he filed a report stating that he was attacked by two Me.109s but had managed to beat them off! In fact all the Pilots concerned seemed quite able to carry on the War without an enemy at all!". Three Pilots were involved plus an Observer – in reality only one of them could have been Prune!

'Lendon' imagined 'Prune' had been called to the Palace for an 'investiture'.

PLATE 3.

PHOTOGRAPH BY TERENCE J. DONOVAN.

'Prune's' patched hat, scarf and battered flying kit actually existed (as replicated above)
and resided next to 'his' desk in Anthony Armstrong's office.
Unfortunately the items were plundered by souvenir hunters at the end of the war.

PLATE 4.

P.O. PRUNE'S GOOD RESOLUTIONS FOR FIGHTER PILOTS

1. I will strain every nerve to improve my marksmanship, realising that the best flying in the world does not actually shoot the enemy down.

2. I will never say anything over the R/T unless I consider it absolutely necessary. I will keep my transmissions as short as possible (not more than 5 sec.).

3. If the R/T packs up: first, I will make certain that the set is switched on and on the correct channel; next I will make certain that my microphone is switched on; then that the plug on my telephone is pushed right home; and lastly that the contactor is OUT. Only after that will I blame the set.

4. When I fly in formation I will not freeze onto the controls; I will always look all around, above, and behind me; and I will watch the tail of my friends to the right and to the left. If I get behind in formation I will weave like Hell: I will never stooge along on a straight and level course, asking to be shot up the tail. (It's so undignified for one thing!).

5. On coming in to land I will not try and be clever by formating closely: I will always keep a safe distance from my leader so that I can look ahead with safety and see there are no obstacles in my path.

6. Before taxying out to take off, I will always see that: (a) the petrol is turned on; (b) the throttle adjusting nut is tight; (c) the flaps are up; (d) the actuating gear is correctly set; and (e) the airscrew (*sic*) is in fine pitch.

7. If on landing I feel I may be overshooting I will not twitter until it is too late, but I swear I will open up and go round again.

8. If I get lost over England and cannot get a vector home, I will land at the first available aerodrome and 'phone base immediately (i.e., before having a quickie in the Mess). I will not wait until I have half a pint of petrol left before I decide I am lost and must force-land.

9. I will always sign the authorisation book and the Form 700; and I will note the letter of the aircraft in which my section leader is flying so that I don't perhaps go off with the wrong chap in the wrong direction.

10. I will always look after my parachute, my dinghy and my helmet, and not drag them in the mud. (Of course, if the parachute won't open due to maltreatment, it can always be exchanged for a new one, but I won't be very interested by then.).

11. In my own interest I will always see that I have fluorescine in my Mae West, that my torch works, and that I have a clip for the dinghy doglead on my Mae West. (I've tried tying the thing to my trousers but it's too much of a strain on the fly-buttons!).

12. Finally – and because I want to live – I promise never to turn away from an attacking aircraft; never to alter my steep turn from one side to the other when evading a Hun; always to look behind me in expectation of a Hun on my tail; never under any circumstance to straggle; never to follow a Hun down with my eyes or my aircraft. (There will be plenty of chances to "confirm" aircraft later on.). "And so, if I have my finger well out all the time, I damn well won't get shot down or boob in any way, so help me, Gawd". – Pilot Officer Prune added that Resolutions like these were asking "a good bit of a fellow", but anything was worth trying.

Attitudes towards the enemy were varied but with the rare exception of one or two, who coldly and implacably held onto a hatred, most Fighter Pilots called them the 'Hun' and refrained from any personal feelings. The enemy was quite simply the opposition and they tore into them as if they were a visiting rugby team from a rival school that honour demanded they flatten. This idea was also shared by the groundcrews but not by the civilian population of Southern England. With a hatred fostered by persistent bombing raids they cursed the enemy as 'Nazis' and, seeing flaming aircraft fall to the ground and explode on impact, were deeply suspicious of anyone descending by parachute. Unaware of the true diversity of the Allies flying in Fighter Command, civilians took to attacking any parachutist who couldn't reply to a challenge in clear, unaccented, English. Thus, Pilots forced to bale out from a damaged aircraft after a sortie found themselves in as much danger from a pitchfork on the ground as they had from the Hun in the air. At first this led to several 'Prunish' incidents but, towards the end of the Battle of Britain, the problem became so severe that the Air Ministry was forced to act and issued an official announcement which had to be repeated on many occasions:

"During air battles over Britain our Fighter Pilots often have to land by parachute after baling out of damaged aircraft. While the necessity for public vigilance in regard to parachute landings continues, it is emphasised that force should not be used unless parachutists adopt a threatening attitude or attempt hostile acts. Not only is it likely that the isolated parachutist may be a British fighter pilot, but he may well be one of our Polish, Czechoslovak, French, Belgian or Dutch allies who cannot speak English. Also the Pilot may be wounded, injured by a bad landing, or exhausted and unable

A spot of Typhoon trouble on the ground at No. 56 OTU.

to answer questions quickly or clearly. The greatest care and discretion should be shown before assuming that a parachutist is an enemy".

In addition to those European Allies, Commonwealth (Canadian, New Zealand, South African, Australian) and American accents were much in evidence in Fighter Command – this sometimes led to great confusion, especially for Prune when he had to explain the result of his latest escapade on the telephone and mistakenly believed he had been put through to Berlin.

"Our average day is from dawn to dusk
Which doesn't sound much I'll admit,
But when dawn is at three and dusk is at ten
You'll agree it's a bit of a s—t!"

(32 Squadron - 1941)

BOMBER COMMAND

Bomber Command presented a nasty shock for Pilot Officer Prune, posted as he had to be (in line with 'Tee Emm's' training policy) to all Commands simultaneously. Suddenly surrounded by an 'army' of people, Prune was no longer the individual in a single-seat fighter but, as Pilot, he had become the Captain of the aircraft and was expected to be a leader of a team within a team. Whereas a Fighter Squadron comprised some twenty-four pilots plus groundcrew, and most people knew each other by name, a Heavy Bomber Squadron contained a minimum of 140 Aircrew plus the much larger groundcrews and a retinue of specialist non-flying personnel. An average Squadron in Bomber Command consisted of two Flights of eight aircraft, two reserve aircraft and four additional crews – with two Squadrons usually based at the same station, the total number of personnel could reach two thousand. Unlike the Fighter 'Boys' the Bomber Crews, as much as was possible, formed into a team at their OTU (Operational Training Unit) and remained together for a tour of duty which was designated as 250 operational hours (later increased to 300) or 30 operations. An 'op' counted only if the aircraft had reached target before returning and crews, on the completion of their tour, would usually opt for a stand down of between six months and a year at an OTU before being posted back to a fully operational Squadron. Those who completed two full tours of duty would then be designated non-operational. There were those 'War Lovers' who wished to continue for a second tour immediately, and those who requested a third tour. Towards the end of the War an option was given to extend for 45 operations (in parity with the Pathfinder Force) against a longer period in a non-operational capacity but at the same time a full operation depended on how far East it was flown and shorter missions counted as fractions in the 'Tour Tally'. Bomber crews flew only when operations were designated and would attend briefings or attend to practice and training in the intervening periods which could be days, or even a week.

A Heavy Bomber crew was initially made up of a Pilot, a Co-Pilot, a Navigator/Bomb Aimer, a Wireless Operator/Air Gunner, and one or two Air Gunners depending on the aircraft. But by March 1942, which marked the real expansion of Bomber Command with four-engine heavy bombers such as the Lancaster, significant changes were made in the format and workloads of the crews. The introduction of an Auto-Pilot enabled the scrapping of the Co-Pilot - which released a large number of fully trained Pilots for operational duties as Captains. The reliability of a Ground Controlled Approach system also helped with this decision. The increasing complexity of the aircraft and the management of its systems created the new role of Flight Engineer who would act as assistant to the Pilot. The Navigator, also with a massively increased workload due to 'technological advances', was freed from the role of Bomb Aimer which (to be drawn from those who had done some Pilot training) became a role on its own. And, the Wireless Operator, whose activities had also undergone significant development, was freed from his Air Gunner duties. The effect was to increase the average crew size from six to seven (some heavy bombers carried eight). This increase in aircrew requirement was, however, offset by a reduction in the time taken to train individuals; because, with the exception of the Flight Engineer, each crew member now could concentrate on developing a single skill - although, if in trouble, crew members still took to doubling up on critical tasks. In a structure such as this there were

'Bomber Boys', briefed and ready, clamber aboard the transport out to their aircraft.

Pilot and Flight Engineer in the cockpit of a No.7 Squadron Stirling.

advantages as well as disadvantages for Pilot Officer Prune. At least now he could simply concentrate on flying the aircraft but, back at 'Tee Emm', Anthony Armstrong had a problem since his brief was to cover all aspects of Bomber Command aircrew training. There was only one solution, Prune had to have his own crew with each member possessing a brand of 'inanity' which matched their Captain's. Enter 'Flying Officer Fixe' the Navigator, 'Sergeant Backtune' the Wireless Operator, 'Sergeant Straddle' the Bomb Aimer and Sergeants 'Winde' and 'Burste' Air Gunners. The Flight Engineer was omitted from this motley cavalcade largely because the crew came together, by the accident of necessity, over a period of time through the pages of 'Tee Emm' as and when an article required such a character for its presentation. And, because the

more technical material that was the 'stuff' of Flight Engineers was in a higher scrutiny classification than 'Tee Emm's' 'Official Use Only'.

Before the advent of the 'Heavies' and Bomber Command's dramatic expansion, the mainstay of the Command had been with medium/light twin-engine aircraft and the ill fated single-engine 'Battle'. With the exception of the Battle a certain number of medium/light Squadrons remained and were detailed to more specialised 'tactical' daylight operations, such as 'Rhubarbs', often in co-ordination with Fighter Command. During 1940 and 1941 bombing statistics had proved disastrous, a mere 20 per cent of aircraft reaching or finding their designated targets and, of those, even fewer dropping their loads with accuracy. The

GROUND CONTROLLED APPROACH

W. HOOPER.

appointment of Air Vice-Marshal Arthur T. Harris to Air Marshal, Air Officer Commanding-in-Chief, Bomber Command, in February 1942 was to signal the change. AM Harris favoured the new 'Heavies' that were coming on line and to demonstrate the Command's potential effectiveness, he decided to mount three massive raids against principal German cities. Utilising every bomber he could lay his hands on, AM Harris dispatched 1,000 aircraft for a night raid against Cologne on the 30/31st of May. The publicity and propaganda secured by this and the subsequent raids on Essen and Bremen achieved the desired effect and AM Harris received the green light to structure Bomber Command into the massive 'offensive' force it became. Training had to be the keynote. Not only had the crews increased in size in a rapidly expanding force but there was the equally rapid development of technological aids to contend with. Pumping through the sheer number of personnel required was in itself a mammoth task but very often a Mk.2 instrument could be replaced by a Mk.4 with different operating procedures by time a 'chap' had completed his time at an OTU, let alone at HCU (Heavy Conversion Unit). AM Harris was all for these aids; the bombing statistics had to be improved and anything that would help accuracy to the target, at the target and effect a safe return was looked at,

analysed, tested and, if proven, introduced. Here 'Tee Emm' with Pilot Officer Prune and his newly-established crew had a role to play. Not only could 'Tee Emm' continue with its usual flight safety material and its general 'gee up' to Aircrew on training pointers and other matters but it could introduce changes in equipment and its use, reminding the specialists to pay attention to the more technical information available elsewhere.

One of the main attributes to be acquired by Aircrew in Bomber Command was stamina. Unlike Fighter Command which, even with its deepest 'sweeps' into France, never expected its Pilots to be in the air for more than one and a half hours, Bomber Command crews could find themselves airborne for up to nine hours on an operation. (Prune had his own method of dealing with this – see above). Admittedly Bomber Crews were not required to fly sorties day-after-day but the nature of their work required a great deal of careful planning and therefore briefing. In addition to which, they were weather-dependent both for the trip itself and while over the target zone. This could mean hours and sometimes days of hanging around the airfield, cut off from the outside world by a security clampdown, being rebriefed and waiting for operational clearance. The nature of tension among Bomber crews was inevitably different from that of the 'Fighter Boys' and 'Bomber Boys' were thought to be more serious minded. A popular conception of

the time was that Fighter Pilots smoked cigarettes whereas Bomber Pilots puffed on a pipe – none of which was strictly true. The endurance of a long flight out, a tense period over target in which any action could only be defensive and a long flight

Bombing up a Lancaster prior to a night raid.

TEN LITTLE BOMBER BOYS

Ten little Bomber boys off to strafe the Rhine,
One went to Hamburg and then there were nine.
Nine little Bomber boys, one of them was late,
Went and taxy-ed out too fast and then there were eight.
Eight little Bomber boys all their engines revving,
One retracted undercart and then there were sevving.
Seven little Bomber boys, one knew all the tricks,
Cut through the balloon barrage and then there were six.
Six little Bomber boys eager to arrive,
One over-boosted and then there were five.
Five little Bomber boys crossed the hostile shore,
One flew level through the flak and then there were four.
Four little Bomber boys, one came down at sea,
Didn't know his dinghy drill and then there were three.
Three little Bomber boys homing on the "Q".
One took QDR for QDM and then there were two.
Two little bomber boys not thinking of the Hun,
Forgot about intruders and then there was one.
One little Bomber boy eager to be done,
Overshot, did not go round and then there was none.
No little Bomber boys left to shoot a line
Of those huge fires left burning at those targets on the Rhine,
And ten expensive aircraft will never fly again
With their ten expensive aircrews who took so long to train.

W. HOOPER R.A.F.

home possibly with a damaged aircraft did, however, tend to produce a more soul searching type of character. Fighter Pilots freely discussed their sorties but Bomber Crews seldom talked about their raids, no matter what had happened. Rather, they were thankful to have returned safely and glad to be able to tick yet another mission off their 'Tour'.

After the critical period of take-off, with most of the crew huddled amidships and engines straining under a full load of fuel and bombs, a Bomber Pilot's first priority was to attain the allotted altitude and to maintain his position in a darkening sky. Thereafter his role was to keep the aircraft on course as instructed by the Navigator. And, to reduce the strain of concentration required in following a track that would be anything but straightforward (let alone 'weaving' and 'jinking' to avoid detection, 'Flak' and enemy night fighters) the aircraft would be fitted with an Automatic-Pilot. 'George', the familiar form of address for a

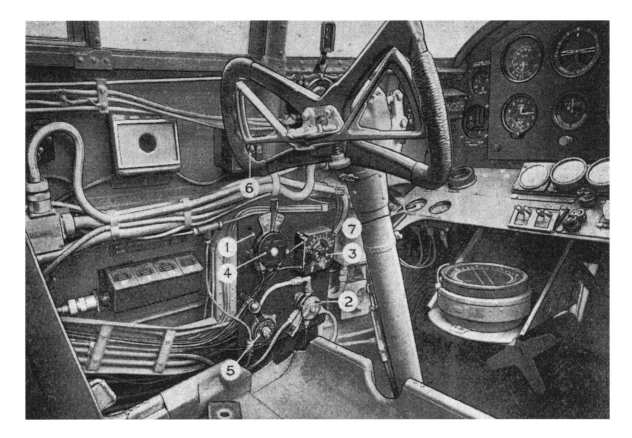

The mysterious and wonderous component workings of 'George' the Automatic Pilot.

stranger in early RAF slang, was the popular name of this device and had been given this usage as early as 1931. Automatic-Pilots of varying degrees of sophistication had been around for some years but their introduction into the RAF was a deliberate move to reduce and spread workloads as well as

Prune found he could overpower "George".

adding a safety factor in certain emergency situations. Some Pilots relished 'George' while others hated 'him', but the truth was he could almost always fly a more accurate course than his human counterpart. As late as February 1943 Pilots were still not using 'George' to 'his' best advantage and 'Tee Emm' made the point: "He does not worry about cloud bumps or dirty weather, and when you know him he can be a real friend. 'And anyone,' as P.O. Prune says, 'who does my work for me, is a friend of mine!'" The introduction of the much simplified Mk. VIII in late 1944 produced a riot of 'unserviceable autopilot' reports on the infamous 'Form 700'. Most were due to confusion in operation and Anthony Armstrong attempted to set the record straight. "Pilots are naturally but human and so tend to prefer a gadget to which they are used, rather than a new gadget. But that's no excuse for not giving something a proper trial. Especially when that new gadget is really a better gadget – or, if it isn't, what the hell's the use of the Research people?". Whether 'Tee Emm's' stab at the problem worked is unknown but 'George' was always depicted as an alien invisible man dressed in flying kit and Anthony Armstrong signed off on the subject with "The fault, dear Prunus, lies not in our George but in ourselves".

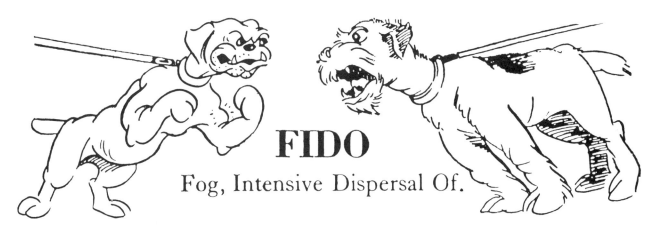

FIDO

Fog, Intensive Dispersal Of.

Another great aid to the Bomber Pilot was FIDO which although it wasn't fully established until mid-1944, was nevertheless responsible for saving a considerable number of lives. The problem of fogbound airfields, particularly for the returning Bomber which might be badly damaged and short of fuel, was playing havoc with Bomber Command Operations planning. One particular disaster had upset AM Harris and dented the morale of Bomber Crews when "large numbers of aircraft returning from a gruelling sortie had found nowhere to land and scores had crashed to destruction in the fogbound English countryside". AM Harris referred the matter to the Air Ministry who referred it to the Ministry of Aircraft Production. Lord Cherwell, the Scientific Adviser to the Prime Minister, was advised and in late 1942 brought it to the attention of Winston Churchill. The Prime Minister immediately contacted Geoffrey Lloyd of the Petroleum Warfare Department who set his 'boffins' to work. Lloyd wasn't long in coming up with an answer but time was needed for experiment.

The solution was to run a series of pipes 50 yards along each side of a runway for at least 1,000 yards, pumping petroleum under pressure and burning-off vaporised fuel (smokeless) at regular intervals. Group Captain D.C.T. Bennett was the first to try a practical landing in a Lancaster with FIDO burning at the initial installation at Gravely. Based on this and subsequent tests in 200 yards of visibility it was reported as a great success, "the intense heat generated cut a chasm through the fog which could be seen from above and the aircraft could fly down into this chasm and land on the runway". After which, key airfields in the main Bomber areas (and later Coastal Stations) were equipped to provide safe points of return. 'Tee Emm' took on the task of conveying confidence in the system to Bomber Pilots and personalised FIDO as a rival to Prune's dog 'Binder'. By VE- Day, "some 2,486 aircraft were landed with FIDO's aid", and it was recorded that the use of FIDO had increased the frequency of operation of the Path Finder Force by more than 30 per cent.

A 'FIDO' landing amid the burners at Gravely Airfield.

Navigation Pointers.

The Navigator, although not the Captain, was in reality the most important member of a Bomber crew. He could often be of higher rank than the Pilot (ie: Flying Officer Fixe with Pilot Officer Prune), although rank didn't count in the air and the Captain of an aircraft was always its ultimate Commander. During the early days of the War the Navigator only had his watch, a compass, radio fixes from directional scanning of set beacons and astro fixes from the position of the stars to help him plot his position on the chart. In addition to which, he was expected to move forward when approaching target and guide the Pilot to the exact point at which the Navigator would release the bomb load. All of this was strictly weather-dependent and confirmation of an Estimated Position plotted on the chart could only be made by visual reference. This severely reduced the operational possibilities of Bomber Command and placed a huge reliance on accurate sightings at night to ensure the correct target was hit. A complicated and tactical course planned at Operations Briefing was very often changed in flight by updated intelligence or revised meteorological information. On-route encounters with enemy aircraft or diversions demanded by unexpected anti-aircraft defences also helped to disorientate an unwary Navigator. Accuracy in map reading, careful calibration of wind drift and the variance of air/ground speeds as well as practise in visual sightings from altitude were vital.

During the first year of its publication, 'Tee Emm' scarcely mentioned navigation but, in early 1942, coinciding with the expansion of Bomber Command, it began to tackle the subject. AM Harris was adamant that accurate navigation and a release from weather dependency were the two factors that would dramatically turn the corner in the effectiveness of Bomber Command. The latter had to await suitable scientific development but the former could be tackled immediately and the pressure was on for attention to good navigation practice. Wing Commander D. Richardson, based at the Air Ministry, was given the task of rewriting the 'Standard Manual of Air Navigation' and Francis Chichester (shortly to join him as a Flying Officer in the RAFVR) had produced a game called 'Pin Point the Bomber' which established a

W.HOOPER

Prune practises pin-pointing through cloud.

developed during 1941 and by mid-1942 was starting to become available to Bomber Command. The beauty of this system, as far as AM Harris was concerned, was that the limitless number of precise co-ordinates it could supply, with a high degree of accuracy over a 350-400 mile range, spelt the end of, weather-dependency. This should have meant 'Blind Bombing' had become a possibility but 'Gee' had its limitations and suffered from both interference and enemy jamming. 'Oboe' was a further development of 'RDF' which again used ground stations but this time, from signals received, the aircraft was tracked over the target and instructed when to release its bomb load. It did not become operationally available until early 1943 and its accuracy, some 300 yards, was the turning point for Blind Bombing but technical limitations confined its use to 'marker' aircraft. The ultimate device was 'H2S', which bounced 'RDF' signals off the terrain below and received them to build up a continuous enlargeable map picture on a cathode-ray tube. The map required interpretation by the Navigator but, with a 30-40 mile image to work with, 'Blind Bombing' was no longer blind. The development of all this technology transformed the art of navigation in Bomber Command but until 1944 the average Navigator only had 'Gee' which still depended on good chartwork. Therefore 'Tee Emm' continued to emphasise the importance of accuracy in DR (Dead Reckoning) navigation, including visual compass fixes and the taking of astro sights. It also underlined the importance of the Pilot/Navigator relationship and called for Bomber Pilots, especially Prune, to take note.

more thorough approach to map reading and was well received by the 'Top Brass' at Bomber Command HQ. By August 1942 'Tee Emm' had established 'Navigation Pointers' as a regular feature and Anthony Armstrong was busy putting into 'Tee Emm's' style articles written by FO Chichester dealing predominantly with both accurate map reading and the importance of a carefully worked up 'Air Plot'.

'Gee', an 'RDF' ('Radar') navigation device based on disparate ground station signals, had been

The Navigator hard at work in his 'Office'.

The 'Bomb Aimer' at his position in a Lancaster.

The 'Bomb Aimer', or Air Bomber as he was more correctly termed after his role was defined as a member of Aircrew in its own right, worked closely with the Navigator and took over his role once the aircraft was approaching the target zone. Up until that point he was designated to the forward guns, despite a usual lack of formal gunnery training. His precise function, which was to instruct the Pilot so that the aircraft was in the exact position and at the correct speed for accurate bomb release, was essentially always visual – determined by his own sighting of the target or by 'markers' laid by other aircraft. In the Spring of 1942, the Air Ministry suggested to AM Harris that perhaps he should create a special group within Bomber Command whose sole task, exploiting the latest navigation aids, would be to act as 'markers' for the main force of Bombers in a raid. Handpicking the best of the Bomber crews, this group would lay incendiary 'markers' on the exact target position giving the Air Bombers in the Main Force an accurate aiming point for their sights. AM Harris argued against the idea believing that the creation of an elite group might prove devisive; and proposing that if the markers were inaccurate then the whole raid would be wasted. There was truth in his convictions but AM Harris was overruled and the PFF (Pathfinder Force), headed by (now) Air Commodore D.C.T. Bennett (eventually Air Vice-Marshal), was

formed. Combined with improvements in bombsight design, bombing patterns began to get tighter and the Air Ministry view was vindicated.

"Prune is interested in accuracy."

Accurate marking of the target, as AM Harris had underlined, was essential but the introduction of 'Oboe' and 'H2S' dramatically improved 'marker' performance. The 'Bomb Aimer' still had to calculate carefully the wind drift, fall rate times angle against altitude and air/ground speeds in order to set his sights. He also had to 'press the tit' at exactly the right moment but the Pathfinder 'marker' aircraft removed at least one element of doubt. Blind Bombing remained visual by 'skymarking', which represented a series of parachute flares that would burn for some five to seven minutes and were dropped by the Pathfinders to take account of wind drift - the exact target position being determined and given in a calculation of minutes and seconds from their release.

CAN YOU AIM BOMBS—

Command arranged the target,
    The one the Huns prized dearly,
        And Station, Grp. and Sqdn. people
            Gave out the " gen " quite clearly.
                The ground crew checked the aircraft
                    And did a good D.I.
                        The Met man said no front would come
                            To mar the perfect sky.
                                The Armourers put on the bombs
                                    And loaded all the guns.
                                        The Signals Section had arranged
                                            To mystify the Huns.
                                                The pilot steered the courses
                                                    As all good drivers do.
                                                        The F.E. checked his boost and revs.,
                                                            As through the night they flew.
                                                                A. B. and N. had worked as one ;
                                                                    There was no cause to doubt
                                                                        That E.T.A. or T.M.G. could possibly be out.
                                                                            The gunners were quite happy ;
                                                                                Their watch had proved its worth ;
                                                                                    For one of Jerry's " 88s " had
                                                                                        spun its way to earth.
                                                                                            The P.F.F. had marked the spot ;
                                                                                                It really looked a show
                                                                                                    With reds and greens
                                                                                                        cascading
                                                                                                            So clearly there below. . .
                                                                                                                But wasn't it a *pity*—

THROUGH
CARELESSNESS IN
AIMING BOMBS,—
THEY DIDN'T
HIT THE
CITY ?

W. HOOPER.

—OR DO YOU JUST PULL A PLUG ?

Among other duties, which included fusing bombs and operating a target camera to supply Intelligence with the true results of the raid, the 'Bomb Aimer' was usually required (after its introduction in 1943) to 'shovel' out 'Window'. This was a series of aluminium strips dropped in measured quantities at points on route to confuse enemy 'Radar' and upset their night fighter control. Avoiding 'Flak' on the target run was also the 'Bomb Aimer's'

responsibility and he had to instruct the Pilot to 'jink' and 'weave' while not jeopardising a 'clean run' for bomb release. From late 1942, 'Tee Emm', realising the intense workload while under extreme pressure that was the lot of the 'Bomb Aimer', used Sergeant Straddle to lay the "Bad Bombing Bogey". This took the form of emphasising the need for concentration, "there's no point in getting there if you don't get it right".

MARCOLINS !

W HOOPER. R.A.F.

" *Marcolins* : A type of imp or gnome, related to the Gremlin family (*q.v.*) but confining their activities to W/T equipment. Marcolins are small and tubby and appear to be constructed mainly of resistance wire. This enables them amongst other things to insert themselves into the H/T lead and produce a falling feed, otherwise unaccountable. They invariably carry adequate equipment for their purposes, such as soldering irons for shorting positives to negatives, or a monkey-wrench for the double purpose of shifting frequencies or bashing in the tops of valves. Marcolins should be constantly suspected everywhere in W/T equipment and suitable steps taken to discourage and outwit them."

The Wireless Operator both kept the aircraft in touch with Base and acted as an assistant to the Navigator, obtaining fixes from Radio Beacons when required. His prime skill was that of Radio Telegraphist and he would receive and transmit Morse messages which had been encoded either as a series of numeric sequences or as 'Words of the Day'. It was through this system that either a Squadron or an individual aircraft would learn if it had been recalled due to adverse weather conditions or diverted to another target. And, it was via the

Wireless Operator's Morse key that Operations Control would be able to plot the positions of the aircraft and learn how many of the Wing or Squadron had successfully dropped their loads onto target. Obtaining navigational fixes was not easy since the range of the English-based Beacons was often inaudibly stretched when the aircraft flew deeper into the Continent. Even on the return journey, when this type of bearing could become vital, attempts at jamming by the enemy and atmospheric interference could lead to great difficulties.

The Wireless Operator works closely with the Navigator.

Apart from his role as a signaller, he was also in charge of the 'Very' pistol and the 'Colours of the Day', the Wireless Operator acted as an observer. While maintaining a listening watch he would look out through the 'Astro Dome', (a bubble on top of the fuselage designed for the Navigator to take Astro Sights using his bubble sextant), as an extra pair of eyes for the Air Gunners. This role was further developed with 'Boozer', a sweeping signal beam that detected enemy 'Radar' locking onto the aircraft and indicated by a flashing light which was relayed to the Pilot; and 'Monica', a tailwarning transponder that bounced signals off enemy night fighters which were heard as 'blips' on his headset. The advent of 'H2S' considerably refined these tasks and the Wireless Operator was given his own 'H2S' equipment code named 'Fishpond'. Rearward looking, other aircraft in the Bomber stream were shown as constants on the cathode ray tube, and a strange spot of light would be instantly referred to the Air Gunners with information on its bearing and relative approach speed.

Although the Wireless Operator was essentially a signaller and not a radio mechanic, he was nevertheless expected to be able to 'tweak' his apparatus and perform rudimentary running repairs while in flight, using the small kit of spares that was carried. It was not unusual to suffer problems, which is understandable considering the comparative fragility and primitive nature of

electronics during the War. In addition to which, undue vibration could cause short circuits, and damaged aerials and antennas would considerably reduce the strengths of reception and transmission. Sergeant Backtune, Prune's Wireless Operator, suffered badly from 'Marcolins', according to Anthony Armstrong. This was a clever variation of the RAF's famous 'Gremlins' since it covered all the unknown factors that could plague a Wireless

Operator. "Mind your Marcolins" was the theme that 'Tee Emm' thumped while offering sympathy and advice on how to deal with them, albeit psychological rather than electronic. It also pointed out that although they had originated in the Marconi Wireless Telegraphy equipment, hence their name, they had now migrated to the Radio Transmitter.

This sent the Wireless Operator into a frenzy as he was usually the scapegoat for a returning Pilot's discomfort at having to make an unannounced approach instead of being safely vectored into a holding circuit above Base, hopefully by the welcoming and dulcet tones of a WAAF in Air Traffic Control.

FLIGHT ENGINEER: POST WAR

NOW when this war is o'er and done,
Perhaps by nineteen fifty-one,
There'll come a cry from some small lad :
" Tell us a bed-time story Dad ! "

Then sadly reaching from a shelf
A book which notes not dwarf nor elf,
Dad slowly reads from faded leaves
Of Wing Tip and the Vortices.

And other gen the notes unfold
Before the tale is fully told ;
The loss of lift at tip of wing,
Defeated by the Flying Ring.

When cruising for the greatest range
The I.A.S. must never change ;
Except you know when bombs are gone,
And then you choose a lower one.

Economy in mixture strength
Has often been discussed at length ;
Full tanks last longest using " Weak,"
In " Rich " you think they've sprung a leak.

Now bombers are not flown for pleasure
With Revs and Boost fixed at your leisure ;
Boost must be high and Revs quite low,
If flying furthest you would go.

Endurance cruising is a bind,
Its rules stick in the simplest mind.
The first one's short ; you just " Fly Slow,"
The second's shorter still ; " Fly Low."

And now you bear in mind my lad,
What happened to your poor old Dad :
For scoffing at these tales of flight,
He ended up a Stalag mite.

W. HOOPER

The Flight Engineer was largely overlooked by 'Tee Emm' which, in its five years of publication, managed to produce only two items devoted to him - one of which was a rewrite of a technical article about Merlin engines. He was, however, a very important member of the crew and acted as Pilot's assistant throughout flight with responsibility for the management of the aircraft and its systems. Apart from the pre-flight, taxy/power, and take-off 'vital action' checks, which the Flight Engineer did together with the Pilot, his role was to control the engine revs and boost, maintain balance between the engines by setting the propellers' pitch, operate the hydraulics to get the 'undercart' up and select flaps as required by the Pilot. To aid him he sat opposite a bank of myriad dials which read out figures on every aspect of the aircraft, including fuel state, with separate dials showing manifold and oil pressure, temperature, revs and boost for each of the four engines. Take-off was the critical period with a full payload and the Pilot often struggling both with an adverse crosswind and a tendency for the aircraft to try to resort to asymmetric flight. Once in the air, the Flight Engineer's main task was management, particularly of fuel, and he kept a regular log with updated calculations predicting the requirements for a safe return. As the Pilot's assistant he left the aircraft's commander free to concentrate on the complicated evasive flying that was continually necessary to avoid night fighters, 'Flak' and enemy searchlight beams. He also nursed the damaged aircraft home (a Lancaster without ailerons could be made to flat turn quite well using careful adjustment of pitch and revs from one wing to another). As lacking in charisma as his role might have seemed the Flight Engineer remained one of the unsung heroes of Bomber Command, at least as far as 'Tee Emm' was concerned. However it was not unknown for a crippled aircraft to touch down safely, after losing its Pilot, with the 'Bomb Aimer' at the controls and the Flight Engineer at his side.

Bombers Crews take notes at Operations Briefing.

A/C	CAPTAIN	F'GUNNER	TOP GUNNER	TAIL GUNNER	AFFILIATION PRACTISES	COMBATS	SCORE
A	S/LR HUNTER	P/O KNOX	SGT BADGER	F/SGT SCRAPP	x x x x	x x	+ +
B	LT POTT D.F.C	F/O FROST	F/SGT TURNER	SGT DIX	x x	x	+
	F/SGT KEENE	Sgt WATT	P/O WRIGHT	F/SGT PEPPER D.F.M	x x x x x	x x x	+ + +
	P/O PRUNE	P/O DEAFMUTE	SGT BURSTE	SGT WINDE		x !!!	
T	SGT JONAH	SGT NIBBS	P/O POTTS	SGT JAKE	x x x	x x	+

SQUADRON SCORE — DESTROYED / DAMAGED

The Air Gunners, 'Mid-Upper' and 'Tail-End Charlie', were the aircraft's only real defence and their role demanded constant vigilance. "The air gunner is possibly quite the most important member of a bomber crew. In his hands, equally with the air bomber's, is the power to inflict destruction on the enemy; and in his hands, equally with the pilot's, is the ability to bring about the complete destruction of his own aircraft and crew, if he doesn't do his job properly. A pilot who by poor flying crashes his aircraft into a hillside kills his crew without giving them a chance. A gunner who lets an enemy fighter come right up and shoot them down because he can't hit the other fellow first does the same thing".

Tightly encompassed in their 'Perspex' turrets, heavily padded in high-altitude, cold-weather and electrically-heated flying kit, the role of the Air Gunners was an isolated one. The worst position, but often the most critical, was in the tail-end turret. Cut off from the rest of the crew by some 60 feet or so of narrow, confining, fuselage 'Tail-End Charlie' maintained his position from shortly after take-off until landing, during which he was still essential as an observer. Six to eight hours with the only contact via the aircraft's intercom, except a break to use the Elsan if the Captain gave permission, was the limit for a Gunner's endurance bearing in mind the intense concentration required

The 'Tail-End Charlie' isolated in the rear turret of a Lancaster.

to continually scan the night sky. The rear turrets of most bombers carried four .303 Brownings and the mid-upper turret two (towards the end of the War the calibre was increased to .50). These guns had the same rate of fire as those fitted to Fighter aircraft but without the dramatic restrictions of ammunition. The turrets were electrically-controlled and equipped with Gyro sights, empty cartridges were pumped from the breech to fall out of the aircraft via a chute. Air Gunners were also

responsible for getting the aircraft out of trouble when under threat or actual attack. Through the intercom they would instruct the Pilot to make a sharp turn to port or starboard, tell him to 'corkscrew' or 'weave' and the Pilot obeyed these instructions without question.

A very heavy emphasis was laid on Air Gunnery in 'Tee Emm' and Sergeants Winde and Burste were used to hammer home many points as diverse as – the danger of too much oil in the gun mechanism freezing at high altitude or the importance of avoiding shooting-up nearby farmworkers when testing guns on the ground. The main theme was always 'Marksmanship', including pieces on the value of 'Clay Pigeon' shooting which formed an important part of the Air Gunner's initial training and was much encouraged on Bomber Stations as 'good practice' for operational Air Gunners. Anthony Armstrong invented another character called 'F/Lt. Barrell-Ffoulynge, AG' who, in a long running series of letters, wrote to Sgt. Burste, Prune's 'Mid-Upper' Gunner, following him through from OTU into his operational career, offering advice and instruction. Sgt. Winde was Prune's 'Tail-End Charlie' which was just as well as, according to RAF folklore, his name was supposed to be spelt without the additional 'e'.

"Not my left, your left, that's right."

73

to escape from a blazing bomber spinning out of control in a sky filled with 'Flak' could not be expressed satisfactorily. The need for quick thinking and urgent action in such circumstances was left to the human instinct for self-preservation. 'Tee Emm' made the point about the sudden rush of air that would greet exiting Aircrew, "this will take your breath away if you are not ready for it – probably it'll do so even if you are", and emphasised the need for a vital '5 secs', to fall clear of the aircraft (approx 200ft) before attempting to pull the rip-cord. Articles were written explaining landing technique and for those who might be hesitant about jumping Anthony Armstrong added, "it's better to have two feet on the ground in a strange country than to lose your life altogether. After all, those two feet can take you a long way! Even back home!" Successful 'balers out' were entitled to apply to the 'Irvin' (Irving Parachute) company to join the 'Caterpillar Club', membership of which included an official card and a little golden caterpillar badge.

Ditching in the sea was even more of an unknown and whereas dinghy drill could be practised both in the aircraft, on terra firma, and on water in a swimming pool or at sea, a successful ditching

Baling out while on operations and ditching a crippled aircraft in the sea were the two great unknowns that had to be faced as a possibility by Bomber Crews. Parachuting courses were made available later during the War but they were voluntary and there was no time available for operational crews to attend. It was therefore up to 'Tee Emm' to push the idea of constant ground emergency drills and, based on the experiences of those who had done it, to explain what the reality was likely to be. "Every operational crew should practise parachute drill good and hard and often, while safely parked in their own aircraft at dispersal. (P.O. Prune by the way is still in hospital from having done a practice bale out at dispersal and forgetting he wasn't airborne). The best way to get this sort of thing taped is to have each man of the crew in his allotted station in daylight, complete with full flying clothing and with parachute packs correctly stowed". Then 'Tee Emm' suggested, "try it at night, when for once there will be no searchlights, flak or fighters to worry you". The biggest problem was for the Air Gunners who, especially if wounded, might find it difficult to extricate themselves from their turrets and make it to the escape exits in time. Ground drills certainly helped with familiarisation, but the reality of trying

TEN LITTLE AIR CREW BOYS

Ten little air crew boys, bomber types no less,
Ditched in the ocean.   Oh ! what a mess !
One unplugged his intercom, didn't hear a line,
Stayed in his turret ; then there were nine.
Nine little air crew boys, one braced himself too late,
Banged himself upon a spar ; then there were eight.
Eight little air crew boys, one thought he'd swim to heaven,
Dived into the ocean ; then there were seven.
Seven little air crew boys, one's harness all amix,
Got caught in the escape hatch ; then there were six.
Six little air crew boys all glad to be alive,
One overturned the dinghy ; then there were five.
Five little air crew boys, to even up the score,
One missed the rescue line ; then there were four.
Four little air crew boys gaily floating free,
One went and drank salt water ; then there were three.
Three little air crew boys beneath a sky of blue,
One caught a touch of sun ; then there were two.
Two little air crew boys (this tale is nearly done),
Couldn't find the wooden plugs ; then there was one.
One little air crew boy we're very sad to say,
Didn't wear his Mae West.   The corpse turned up to-day.
At the subsequent inquiry this tale there was to tell ;
They'd done their job, a beauty, and they'd pranged the target well ;
Their dinghy drill, it seemed, alone they hadn't studied ;
So all their schemes and hopes and dreams, were well and truly flooded.

related directly to the Captain's skill as a Pilot. Hitting the sea incorrectly was like flying into a concrete mass and the aircraft would break-up and sink immediately. The object was to try and lay the aircraft onto the water by stalling it inches above the waves and in the direction of the prevailing tide or swell but into wind. The crew had to assemble themselves ready for evacuation and in positions that were suitably braced for impact. 'Tee Emm'

again laboured the points about dinghy drill and attempted to portray the reality of ditching an aircraft. It also published a regular series of articles from the much-lauded ASR Service (Air-Sea Rescue), which were packed with useful information on survival and recovery. Like baling out, a successful ditching entitled air crew to become members of the 'Goldfish Club'; this in turn was sponsored by the manufacturers of the survival dinghies (life rafts). Together with a card members received a small goldfish badge which was usually worn on the underside of a member's lapel.

Pigeons were carried by all operational Bomber aircraft (this also applied to Coastal Command long-range sorties) and were an essential item of emergency signalling in addition to a wireless SOS when an aircraft was either abandoned in flight or had to be ditched. Every Bomber Station had an NCO 'pigeon-keeper' who came under the Station Signals Officer and whose job was to maintain an adequate supply of trained homing pigeons for issue to operational crews. Instruction was given in pigeon handling and, primarily, it was the shared duty of the Wireless Operator and the Navigator to take charge and ensure that their aircraft was correctly equipped with a 'waterproofable' pigeon box in case of ditching. Although pigeons were the last resort for communications, they nevertheless held a sense of security for a downed crew whose last Morse message may have just disappeared into the ether. Some 96 per cent of released pigeons arrived back or had their messages picked up and relayed; and that from releases in all weathers and with up to 400 miles of flight. Despite their obvious value, pigeons became the brunt of many jokes and much misuse. 'Cracks' abounded about having 'roundels' painted onto their wing feathers and some were released from returning aircraft that had landed out at another Station with messages of instruction for the Mess or to a Batman about laundry. 'Tee Emm' recalled, " 'No one,' says Prune, 'really takes pigeons seriously.' Well, all we can say is that one day Prune may not think pigeons are quite so funny. A pigeon may, for

Back home for tea, sandwiches and debriefing.

GETTING THERE

instance save his life – that is to say, if it's a broad-minded pigeon who thinks Prune's life worth saving. And from then on, instead of pigeons being funny to Prune, the mere mention of the word 'Prune' in the pigeon loft at night will be the cause of overwhelming twitters of gusty laughter".

The success of a Bomber aircraft was almost entirely dependent on the success of its crew as a team, (even Prune had to knuckle down and pull his weight). The establishment of that team was, however, a completely random process with Pilots, at their OTU, directed to a hangar filled with Navigator, Bomb Aimer, Wireless Operator and Air Gunner OTU graduates, and told to form a crew. Despite this beginning, teamsmanship grew not only out of the fact that the NCOs in a crew (outnumbering the officers) were billeted together but because of the common adversity they shared. And, anyone who didn't 'pull his finger out' would soon find himself licked into shape by the others. Crews became 'comrades at arms' and it wasn't uncommon for either the majority of a crew or a single member to fly more than the allotted number of operations for a tour just to ensure that the crew remained intact for the completion of all its members. A crew also liked to stick with its own aircraft and many a Captain requested a temporary stand down while their aircraft was being made operationally serviceable. Superstition was rife among Bomber crews and nearly every member carried some sort of 'lucky' mascot, even if it was merely one of his girlfriend's stockings wound round his neck, ostensibly to keep out the cold at 15-20,000 feet. Separation from these mascots brought about a sense of gloom and fatality. Certain crew members who'd struck an unlucky patch in terms of association with casualties were considered jinxed, branded with a nickname, and chaps would

THE SUCCESSFUL TEAM

W HOOPER.R.A.F.

do anything to avoid having to fly with them. As ridiculous as this may seem, it presented a very real problem to which the only solution was to post the unfortunate to another Squadron – this was particularly true for Bomber Pilots.

Bomber Command casualties were high and by May 1945, having completed nearly 390,000 sorties, it had lost 10,882 aircraft with a further 5,572 damaged beyond repair. These figures represent a loss of over 55,000 aircrew, of whom nearly one fifth were Canadian, and a further 10,000 prisoners-of-war. In mid-1943, Bomber crews quoted 'Tour Odds' for survival which they rated as seven-to-one until the halfway mark of 15 operations, thereafter the odds shortened to four-to-one for completion – no odds were quoted for a second tour. For their first 'op' a new crew would usually

be sent on a 'milk run' (an easy sortie) which was often 'Gardening' (mine laying). Traditionally the last operation would be similar but that depended on the Squadron CO and whether he could afford to stand down the crew until something suitable came along. The leave allowance for Bomber Crews was six days every six weeks, with 14 days at the end of a Tour prior to posting. The geographical location of many Bomber Stations was remote and crews would usually split up and leave the area for pastures new as a way to relax from the tension of operations. Relaxation on the Station took the form of high jinks in the Mess which often involved the destruction of much furniture and more than few minor injuries. Lost comrades were shrugged-off as having encountered 'a spot of bad luck'; and auctions of their personal possessions, including the ubiquitous 'Bomber Station' bicycle, were

467 Squadron Lancasters preparing for a night raid.

held in the respective Messes with the proceeds to the next-of-kin. The fact that Pilot Officer Prune survived Bomber Command might be attributed to the 'Luck of the Devil' – or, in 'Tee Emm's' case, to yet another posting, for Coastal Command was also in need of his dubious services.

"This bloody Station's a right bloody cuss,
No bloody pubs and no bloody bus,
Nobody cares for poor old bloody us,
Oh, bloody bloody bloody, bloody bloody!"

(12 Squadron - 1943)

OTHER COMMANDS

If Pilot Officer Prune ever had ideas that a posting to Coastal Command meant 'picnics' on the beach, he couldn't have been more wrong. Although it was the smallest of the three principal Home Commands (Fighter, Bomber and Coastal) it was, in many ways, the most demanding and required a particularly high standard of its Pilots and Navigators. It was the first Command to engage the enemy in combat (Sept 4, 1939 when a Hudson of

No. 224 Squadron encountered a Dornier Do 18 flying-boat on patrol out over the North Sea) and already had been mobilised some two weeks before War was declared. Essentially Coastal Command varied between being either a defensive or offensive force whose brief was to be "engaged in the task of protecting merchant shipping and the waters round Britain's coasts". This entailed, "reconnaissance of hostile naval forces and attacks on them when found either at sea or in harbour – attacks on enemy aircraft seeking to attack or destroy our shipping – anti-submarine escort patrols and searches – and mine-laying activities". Its aircraft were both land- and sea-based ranging from Ansons and Hudsons to the purpose-built Beaufort torpedo bombers, Beaufighters, American Catalinas and the massive long-range Sunderland flying-boat. Control of its operations was jointly shared by both the RAF and the Royal Navy, but it was laid down as a principle that the ultimate decision concerning any operation

The crew watch as an 18" torpedo is fitted to their Beaufort.

must rest with the Royal Navy, whose duty it was to fight and win wars at sea. "This did not mean that Coastal Command had no initiative of its own but that the operation requirements of the Admiralty had to come before all else". In practice this was achieved by close co-operation, and Area Combined Operations were staffed by Officers of both services. So far as Coastal Command and the Royal Navy were concerned, there never had been a 'phoney war' but the fall of France in June 1940 meant that the enemy encompassed Britain to the North, East and South. German air and U-boat bases were available from Norway to the Bay of Biscay and, at the same time as Fighter Command had its 'back to the wall' while meeting the threat from the air, Coastal Command was fully stretched trying to keep both the Channel open and to join with the Royal Navy in the Battle for the Atlantic.

In temperament, Coastal Command Pilots and crews resembled their comrades in Bomber rather than Fighter Command. "Their duties have much in common - they involve flights of many hours duration in almost all weathers, and during much of that time the main preoccupation must be whether the aircraft is on its right course or not. Then,

however, the resemblance grows thin. The crew of a bomber are concerned to find a target, which is usually stationary, and to hit it with their bombs; those of an aircraft of Coastal Command have first to find what is very often a moving target and then to hit it, or keep it under observation so that a striking force may do so. Moreover, if they are on convoy protection - and this form of patrol is one of their main duties and entails the spending of many thousands of hours in the air and the covering of many millions of miles over the sea - they may never see a target at all, though they must be constantly on the look-out for one. They are therefore, generally speaking, of the phlegmatic turn of mind. They must find their way by methods of precision, relying on their instruments for guidance. There are no landmarks five hundred miles out in the Atlantic, and they may not see land for nine-tenths of their patrol. There is bred in them much of the sense of direction possessed by the sailor". The ability to Navigate accurately was considered to be one of the most important qualifications in Coastal Command, and crews were trained to have implicit faith in their navigational instruments, particularly the

W.HOOPER.

compass. "To inculcate this requires patience. It is a natural tendency for the eye to look outside the cockpit straining to pick up some solid object which gives a guide to the position of the aircraft". It was for this reason, much to the chagrin of Bomber Command's AM Harris, that Coastal Command staked a claim for development of the new navigational technology 'Gee' and the Magnetron valve used in 'H2S' (which also greatly improved the performance of its ASV, Air to Surface Vessel, developed for anti-submarine work.) Apart from navigation the quality of flying had to be of the highest standard. Torpedo-bombers were required to maintain a steady level course just 50 feet above the sea in order to release the torpedo with an accurate trajectory and often they flew at 'zero' feet from take-off through to attack in order to avoid being detected by enemy 'Radar'. Anti-submarine patrols and convoy escorts were also required to fly continuously at low level and to climb to 2,000 feet was jokingly referred to as 'mountaineering'. Endurance was an everyday part of Coastal Command routine and, especially with the flying-boats, operations could last as long as 18 to 20 hours. To aid some normality in such sorties

both the Catalina and the Sunderland were fully fitted with 'galleys' and hot meals would be prepared and served in flight, usually by a 'Rigger' who was an additional member of these crews. The principal enemies of Coastal Command crews were 'boredom' and the 'weather'. There was no easy way to combat the latter, save by good 'Met' reports which could be suitably interpreted on board, although it is true to say that more Coastal Command aircraft were lost due to adverse weather than to direct action by the enemy. The former was the responsibility of the aircraft's Captain and it was down to him to ensure that a steady routine of reporting and log-keeping kept his crew on the alert.

The men of Coastal Command were proud of their connections with the sea and they found themselves nicknamed 'The Green Bus Line' by members of the other Commands who also referred to Coastal aircraft as 'Kipper Kites'. Flying-boat Aircrew took their connections with the sea to extremes by deliberately exposing their cap badges and tunic buttons to salt corrosion so that they turned green with verdigris, which they steadfastly refused to

W.HOOPER

Ten 18" Torpedoes

TEN 18" TORPEDOES WERE READY FOR THE BRINE,
A STOP VALVE WAS NOT OPEN, AND THEN THERE WERE NINE.
NINE 18" TORPEDOES WOULD SETTLE MOST SHIPS' FATE,
A WATER FLAP HAD NOT BEEN COCKED, AND THEN THERE WERE EIGHT.

EIGHT MK. XII TORPEDOES, SET DEPTH IN FEET, ELEVEN,
ONE WAS SET AT FORTY FEET, AND THEN THERE WERE SEVEN.
SEVEN GOOD TORPEDOES WOULD STILL THE TARGET FIX,
A LANYARD NOT ATTACHED ON ONE, AND THEN THERE WERE SIX.

SIX 18" TORPEDOES, A TIT PRESSED IN A DIVE,
TORPEDO PLUNGED TO SEA BED, AND THEN THERE WERE FIVE.
FIVE, JUST FIVE TORPEDOES, ONE WAS DROPPED WITH YAW,
RESULT WAS FAULTY RUNNING, AND THEN THERE WERE FOUR.

ONLY FOUR TORPEDOES NOW, ALL READY FOR THE SEA,
ONE WAS DROPPED RIGHT OUT OF RANGE, AND THEN THERE WERE THREE.
THREE, BUT THREE TORPEDOES, ONE DROPPED WITHOUT A CLUE,
THE AIRCRAFT WAS NOT LEVEL, AND THEN THERE WERE TWO.

JUST THE TWO TORPEDOES, AND BOTH OF THEM COULD RUN,
MASTER SWITCH FORGOTTEN, AND THEN THERE WAS ONE.
LONELY ONE TORPEDO, AND THAT ONE HIT THE HUN,
BUT IT DIDN'T DO THE DAMAGE THAT TEN FISH MIGHT HAVE DONE.

SO NINE EXPENSIVE WEAPONS WERE WASTED IN THE 'DRINK',
'COS ONLY ONE TORPEDO BOY HAD TRAINED HIMSELF TO THINK.
AND JERRY RAISED HIS STEIN OF BEER AND LAUGHED A LOUD HAW HAW,
HE'D GOT ANOTHER CONVOY THROUGH TO HELP PROLONG THE WAR.

polish even for parade. A love of the sea extended even into spare time activity and it was a group of Officers from the flying-boat base at Calshot Spit who, some years before the War, founded the Royal Air Force Yacht Club. Flying-boat crews were unique in the RAF and the Pilots had to learn the special skill of lifting-off and landing-on a moving surface, taking into account crosswinds, tides, currents and seastate as well as the natural reluctance of the aircraft (due to suction) to break clear of the water. "A great part of their training has a strong naval flavour. They must know almost as much about seamanship as they must know about airmanship. They must be able to handle and control a machine which is both an aircraft and a surface vessel. It is moored to a buoy. It carries an anchor.

Its instruments are calibrated in knots, for speed is calculated in sea, not land, miles and this is so with all aircraft of Coastal Command, whether they are designed to take-off from and alight on land or water".

All of this must have come as a bit of an eye-opener to Pilot Officer Prune whose sole experience with

the 'drink', prior to appearing in Coastal Command, was restricted to bobbing about in his one-man life raft after baling-out over the Channel or shooting-up navigation buoys for a bit of fun (a practice wholly abhorrent to both Trinity House and the Royal Navy). An apocryphal story did the rounds of Coastal Command (everyone swore it was true and it happened to Prune) about the confusion of land and water in the mind of a visiting Air Commodore from HQ to a flying-boat station which was close by an RAF airfield. Insisting on taking over the controls of a Sunderland from its Pilot Officer Captain, the Air Commodore proceeded to demonstrate that he had not lost his touch. The Pilot Officer was less complacent when the Air Commodore closed the throttle, applied two stages of flaps and commenced his descent to the airfield. The Air Commodore refused to listen to the Pilot Officer's protestations but, at the last moment, initiated a go-around eventually making a perfect landing on the nearby designated sea lane. When the engines had been switched off the Air Commodore left his seat and laughed at the Pilot Officer telling him it was just a joke. Then, opening the door in the side of the Sunderland's fuselage, he bid the aircraft's Captian goodbye and stepped out – into thirty-feet of water. In fact, 'Tee Emm' published little material directed specifically at Coastal Command since most of the content aimed at Bomber Command was pertinent to Coastal. Certain exceptions dealt with the problems of 'cuisine' in flight and related to the later generation of aircraft (Liberators and B-17 Fortresses). The Air-Sea Rescue Service did, however, receive regular attention from Anthony Armstrong (see page 75) and from mid-1941 onward Air-Sea Rescue came under the direct control of Coastal Command.

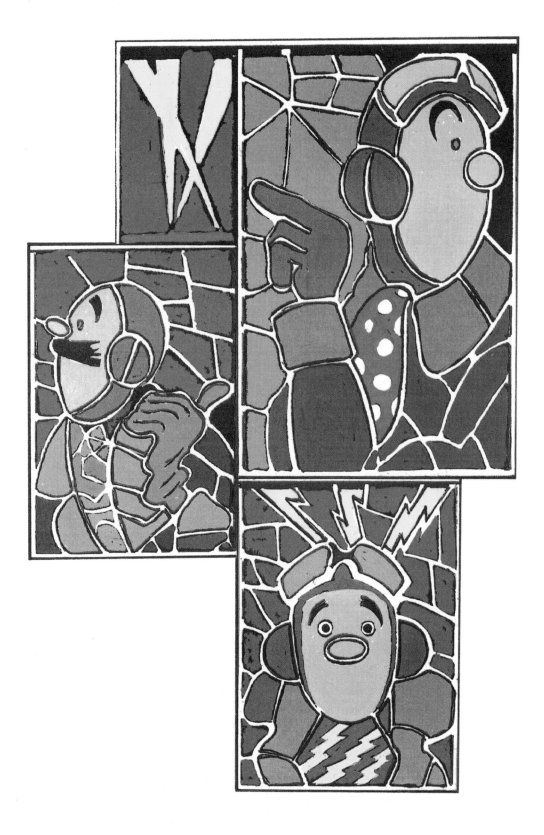

From time to time Anthony Armstrong would strike up in a quasi-religious vein and
present an article as if it were a sermon. Inevitably these contained either Parables or a
series of Commandments. They were illustrated in the style of stained-glass windows
which, due to the nature of 'Tee Emm', were originally only published in black and white.

A Prune Memorial Stained-Glass Window.

PLATE 5.

Prune's desk in Anthony Armstrong's Office as remembered by Peter Endsleigh Castle.

PLATE 6.

Every so often operational Aircrew would be 'stood down' for a rest period, some would go to OTUs as instructors while others, usually the more senior of the Officers would be given a desk job. Often this would be at some Department of the Air Ministry where their practical experience could be put to some advantage. Desk jobs were regarded by Aircrew as only suitable for 'Wingless Wonders' but they were nevertheless important and very often helped with a move upwards on the promotion scale – the ability to organise and delegate being seen as important as good leadership. It was therefore up to 'Tee Emm' to promote such ideas as 'the attributes of good organisational ability' and 'the necessary evaluation of the various elements essential in balanced decision-making'. In early 1942 the RAF Staff College reopened with courses on various aspects of staff work, these were both voluntary and obligatory, depending on an Officer's posting, but any serious-minded RAF careerist was well advised to attend. Anthony Armstrong defined Staff Work as being on three distinct levels: "High level – deals with plans, composition and strategic disposition of the Air Force"; "Low level – concerned with ensuring that letters are sent to the people responsible for and competent to deal with the subject"; and, "Medium

level - deals with marshalling facts and arguments and producing memorandums in which all the relevant facts are stated accurately and in a logical sequence". It was at this 'Medium level' that 'Tee

BIG FLEAS

Big fleas have little fleas
Upon their backs to bite 'em.
Little flees have lesser fleas,
And so ad infinitum.

W. HOOPER.

High Level Staff Work at an Air Council meeting.

Emm' pushed home its message in a semi-regular series of articles which varied from 'Organisation Without Tears' to 'Bumph Speaking'. The latter series was titled after the catchphrase of Jack Train's comic German 'Funf' ("dis is Funf Speaking") in the Tommy Handley Radio Show - 'Bumph' being well-worn military slang for paperwork. Pilot Officer Prune always appeared in these articles - as if Prune, of all people, could ever hope to get organised or for that matter promoted.

But, Anthony Armstrong, stuck behind a desk himself in a hierarchy of rules and regulations, saw the funny side of it and used Prune to his best effect. " 'Staff work!' exclaims Pilot Officer Prune, laughing very heartily. 'Staff work!' he repeats, putting a most offensive accent on the second word. He then murmurs something jovial about 'passengers in the boat' and stops reading this article in favour of the day's 'Jane'. And who shall say he is wrong? Not us – we're 'Jane' fans too".

In fact both of 'Tee Emm's' series of articles were so successful that they gradually broadened their appeal, not only to those who had to face 'office work' for the first time but with general points of principle that applied to everyone in a leadership capacity on operational service. "Do see that your orders are brief, complete, and unambiguous. See that your orders are understood. Remember the story of the Chief Instructor who rushed out of the watch office and grabbed one of his Instructors! 'Didn't I tell you,' he said, 'to see that your pupil did not taxy over that bit of bad ground?' 'I did tell him, sir,' stammered the other, 'but he must have misunderstood me.' 'Only a fool can't make himself understood,' the Chief Instructor roared. 'Do you understand?' 'No, sir,' replied the Instructor, and the C.I. went thoughtfully back to the watch office". Anthony Armstrong, with his own campaign to 'de-Whitehallese' written material, was on home ground when it came to the presentation of the written word and he pushed hard for simple, straightforward communication. But, often ambiguity was used as a deliberate disguise for either indecision or for the refusal to accept

responsibility to take a positive course of action. That, however, was politics and an area in which 'Tee Emm' held no brief. It was more important to get over the message of the vital importance of good Staff Work, and 'Tee Emm' succinctly expressed it thus: "it is not an end in itself, a piece of machinery revolving happily but not connected up to anything at all. It has but one object: to make everything as easy as possible for the operational crews and their ancillaries to defeat the enemy. Staff work, in short, is the method by which the business of war is conducted. A civilian business run without method rarely survives for long. It, however, only ends up in Carey Street: failure for us in the business of war would be a trifle more inconvenient".

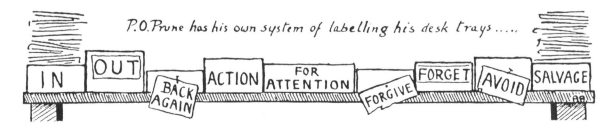

P.O. Prune has his own system of labelling his desk trays.....

IN | OUT | BACK AGAIN | ACTION | FOR ATTENTION | FORGIVE | FORGET | AVOID | SALVAGE

The Women's Auxiliary Air Force had absolutely nothing to do with 'Tee Emm'. None of them were Aircrew and, although WAAFs posted to a Sector Operations Room or working in a Secretarial capacity with an Officer who was on the mailing list may well have thumbed through its contents, it contained nothing which related to their role in the RAF. All that aside, Anthony Armstrong was no 'slouch' when it came to appreciating the value of the 'fair sex', especially where Aircrew were concerned. In early 1942, when he came to writing a piece on smartening-up appearances (particularly uniform) he chose a WAAF as the motivating example. Drawing a comparison between two (fictional?) visitors to his office, Anthony Armstrong continued: "they both wore RAF uniform; and the difference (apart from the main fact that one was a woman and one a man, if you know what we mean) was in the way they wore that uniform. Our first visitor was A.C.W.2 Winsum. ("What ho!" says P.O. Prune.) She seemed to our eyes to be as smart as smart, her uniform was

WAAFs on the March in a 'Wings for Victory' parade.

correct and well kept as any we've seen. Of course there may have been a detail or so that a W.A.A.F. Officer might have cavilled at, but we wouldn't know. To tell the truth, we weren't looking at the uniform all the time. 'Waff Winsum', it seemed had come into our office in error. She had a car outside in which she thought we wanted to go to a station in Hertfordshire. She was right in one respect. We did want a car. We are always wanting cars - to go to Stations in Hertfordshire, or, indeed, any Station that car happens to be going to. But our trouble is, we never get cars, and A.C.W.2 Winsum's instinct pretty soon diagnosed that fact. In spite of our attempt to put across the idea that we were a bosom friend of the Very Senior Officer who had ordered the car and who wouldn't in the least mind a dear old pal having it instead, she sized us up as an insignificant form of lower commissioned life and went out of our world, leaving an impression of attractive and efficient smartness that stayed with us like a breath of fresh air in our musty old office". Having accidentally invented a new character for 'Tee Emm' and lit up Prune's eyes, it seemed obvious to keep the idea running. "P.O. Prune had

just remarked reminiscently that 'that' was just his piece of cake and he'd like to see more of 'Waff Winsum', why not get her on 'Tee Emm' staff?".

" Your pitot-head cover, sir."

There was, however, an initial uneasy relationship between the Women's Auxiliary Air Force and the Royal Air Force, despite there having previously been a 'Women's Royal Air Force' (disbanded in 1920). Although both WAAF and RAF came under the Air Ministry, they were separate organisations with their own codes of discipline and the WAAF brief was simply: "the substitution of women for Royal Air Force personnel in certain appointments and trades in the RAF". Women were recruited according to their civilian skills; their Officers were appointed rather than commissioned, and there was no question of WAAF personnel being given flying duties. There was also an initial unease, reflected by both Officers and NCOs, at women on an RAF Station doing work that was usually done by a man. "Three WAAFs who had pilots certificates were taught to be Link Trainer instructors. But, though thoroughly competent in their work, their use was restricted by a genuine prejudice. Several would-be pilots objected, not so much perhaps at being taught to fly by a particular woman, than to the thought that it had been left to a WAAF to teach them to fly". The expansion of the Women's Auxiliary Air Force soon changed such ideas and WAAFs were seen everywhere and much lauded for their diligence. Even so, they strove to keep to themselves with their own separate quarters, messes (both Officers and NCOs), exercise areas and recreation rooms. Fraternisation between WAAFs

People wrote to Prune as though he existed, so why not develop the personal side of his life? Prune would only reflect the thoughts of most Aircrew as they observed the increasing number of WAAFs serving in many different capacities on RAF Stations.

At work on a target model in Bomber Command and the specially photographed Recruitment Image.

and members of the RAF was frowned upon, and although many relationships and marriages did spring up they were strictly off-duty affairs. Every effort was made to get RAF personnel, especially Aircrew, to accept WAAFs as fellow workers regardless of their sex. Anthony Armstrong's presentation of 'Waff Winsum' went against that code, which had been carefully set by the WAAF Directorate in conjunction with the Air Member for Personnel, and accordingly he soft-pedalled the idea. Nevertheless, he took pains to keep his character alive and 'Waff Winsum' cropped up as a passing mention in several articles throughout 1942-43 and the first half of 1944.

The first illustrations of 'Waff Winsum' were drawn by 'Lawson', a well-known book illustrator and it wasn't until late 1943 that Bill Hooper, following on from Lawson's portrayal, added her into a Prune drawing. By mid-1944 attitudes to the WAAFs had changed dramatically, both at Air Ministry level and with RAF personnel. Women had replaced some 15 different RAF Officer

categories and were working in 59 different Airman trades (compared with the 18 they restricted to in 1940), although they were still confined to non-combatant duties. Mixed accommodation and mixed messes had become more commonplace, out of practical necessity, and WAAFs, although remaining secondary to their male counterparts in terms of pay and ration allowances, were accepted as a vital component of the Royal Air Force. With the original code of fraternisation no longer the strong moral issue it still was in 1942, Anthony Armstrong felt the time was right to 'air' 'Waff Winsum' again and in 'Tee Emm's' fantasy film scenario of September 1944, entitled 'This Side of the Ocean', he gave 'Waff Winsum' second billing to Pilot Officer Percy Prune. The object of this piece of light fiction, apart from satirising the cliched style of many of the Hollywood films of that period, was to show a totally different side of Prune. One in which, for a change, he did everything right and received the appropriate praise. The story commenced with Prune, having been severely ragged by his comrades in the Mess, determined to

three years ago now since he first met her. Ah, the memory of that meeting! It was while his aircraft was being serviced and Prune was still in the cockpit when a slender boyish figure passed him carrying a bit of cowling and with an oily smudge on her arm. Prune took one look at her and the general effect on him was as of a chap shot through the heart – as indeed he metaphorically was. He just stared and stared dazedly, occasionally muttering 'Wizard' or 'Good Show!' to himself until finally aroused by a fitter tapping him on the shoulder and intimating that it was about time he took part in the war again. It was, as he himself put it, love at first sight". Then rounding it all off with a 'happy ever after' line Anthony Armstrong announced 'Tee Emm's' congratulation to all three of them. "Yes, all three, we said; for it is just over a year ago that the Prune-Winsum nuptials were first celebrated, though it has been up till now kept secret, and the union has been blessed by a little Peter Prune".

Although the Royal Air Force had 'two Easts', Middle East Command (North Africa and the Mediterranean) and Air Command, South-East

demonstrate his true capabilities and, in smart, clean and unadulterated uniform, he sets out to impress everyone by doing everything right, and by displaying more than his fair share of valour. During this 'fictional' day he turns to 'Waff Winsum', "looking attractively workmanlike in her overalls – and makes a date for that night behind 'dispersal'". On his return from the operation (Bomber Command) he receives the DFC from a VIP and is informed of his immediate promotion straight to Flight Lieutenant. Then comes the love interest, "Prune is seen making rapidly for that date behind dispersal where 'Waaf Winsum' awaits him, newly permed, wearing her best silk stockings, only too eager to congratulate, if not reward, her hero. The film fades out in the usual clinch: P.O. Prune versus 'Waff Winsum'. Her kisses are on his lips (see page 92). In letters of fire across the screen we read: 'Receiving his just reward' ". Of course it all turned out to be a dream and Prune was seen once again in his true light.

'Waff Winsum' appeared briefly in January 1945 in a short article about recreational activities but it wasn't until the final issue of 'Tee Emm', in March 1946, that Anthony Armstrong tied-up the story and announced that Prune, much as had been expected, had 'gone for a feminine Burton'. "It is

Asia (Malaya, India and Burma), it was to the latter that 'Tee Emm' addressed itself and then not until February 1944. In many respects the RAF's War in the Far East had become a forgotten War. Following the attack on Pearl Harbor in December 1941 and the subsequent attack and invasion of Malaya in January 1942, the Japanese began their sweep to the West. Moving across Burma, their intention was to protect their gains in the South-West Pacific; cut off China from her western supplies; and,

having consolidated their position, to prepare to mount an invasion of India. British and Allied Forces had been pushed back to a defensive line that extended from the borders of India and Burma across the north of French Indo-China into the Chinese mainland. Valiant actions had been fought by the RAF, not only in support of the retreating Allied Armies but with offensive actions, such as Sumatra and Java, that attempted to stem the further expansion of the enemy's strongholds. There the

The RAF working alongside the Indian Air Force.

RAF fought to the finish with the majority of survivors taken as prisoners-of-war. Throughout 1942 and 1943 the RAF, flying fighters, bombers and transports, fought alongside the USAAF and the Indian Air Force (mainly transports) both to aid the defensive positions (with short sharp attacks behind the Japanese lines) and to provide supplies and air support for the troops on the ground. Often ill-equipped and facing vastly superior odds the RAF, despite its major efforts being concentrated on the War in Europe, used the two years to strengthen its resources both in manpower and machines. Most importantly, with the newer modifications of aircraft that were not only better suited for the climate but had increased performance and could match or even improve on those flown by the Imperial Japanese Air Forces. In November 1943, British and American Forces amalgamated under a new South-East Asia Command which incorporated 52 RAF Squadrons and combined the air transport and supply Squadrons into a 'Troop Carrier Command' under a USAAF Brigadier-General. By the beginning of 1944 the Allied Forces in Europe had gained the upper hand and it made sense to transfer experienced Aircrew to South-East Asia to fulfil the requirements. Timing proved provident for, in February 1944, the Japanese launched a revised offensive with the aim of breaking through and taking the North of India. The initial success of the Japanese initiative was soon turned around by the Allied forces aided by massive support from the SEAC air services, both in continual supply of the ground troops and by the ceaseless bombing and strafing of every possible Japanese target ahead of the Infantry. After six

months of relentless attacks, both on the ground and from the air, the Japanese Army found itself in retreat back through Burma. This was to be a slow but ongoing process throughout the rest of 1944 and on into 1945.

'Tee Emm's' role, apart from the coincidence that its supreme champion AM Garrod (now Air Marshal Sir Guy) had just been posted to Air Officer Commanding-in-Chief, South-East Asia Command, was to publish a series of articles on the relative differences between the Far East and European Theatres of War. Under the banner of 'Flying Out East', Anthony Armstrong rewrote into 'Tee Emm's' style several pieces which explained what Aircrew might expect to find, if and when they got out there - pointing up some of

Brewster Buffalo Pilots of 67 Squadron at Mingaladon in Burma.

the more delightful aspects to a posting 'away from it all':

Aircraft: "All the types of aircraft you'll fly out there will have been originally designed for more temperate climates, which means that in hot ones they won't operate at maximum efficiency. Almost certainly you'll be disappointed with your aircraft's performance; firstly, because the engines don't deliver the power that they would in cooler air, and, secondly, because you don't get as much 'lift' from the atmosphere as you do in England. Moreover, the additional radiators, oil coolers and other tropical gadgets detract from performance".

Heat: "The metal parts of an aircraft get so hot that to touch them is about as comfortable as fondling a stove in full blast – if you had a piece of bacon you could fry sausages and bacon on a Spitfire, if you had any sausages".

The Enemy: "A wily and dangerous foe. He believes in supreme sacrifice at the altar of his Emperor and will literally fight to the last man though he is not the suicidal maniac some people would lead us to believe".

Weather: "All the existing types hotted up a trifle and shuffled, so you never quite know what to expect anywhere at anytime, plus deluges that penetrate into every cranny as easily and persistently as moth into your laid-by civvy suit – this makes fabric or plywood, or glued joints deteriorate extraordinarily quickly".

Dust: "During the dry season what little grass there may have been on the airstrip wilts, and soon fails entirely to bind the surface. Aircraft taking off leave behind them a huge wall of dust which usually blankets the strip, Flight-Tents and even adjacent Erks in a very commendable imitation of a sand storm".

Insects: "Take a great deal of interest in aircraft. Many of them seem to look on cockpit instruments as a home from home - one species of wasp actually seems to include Pitot heads in its normal life cycle – it is also very advisable to shake out your flying clothing and helmet before putting them on. Things like scorpions have a great fancy for curling up inside for a quiet zizz and hate being disturbed. Having a flea in the ear is nothing to having a scorpion in it!".

LIVE TO FIGHT ANOTHER DAY

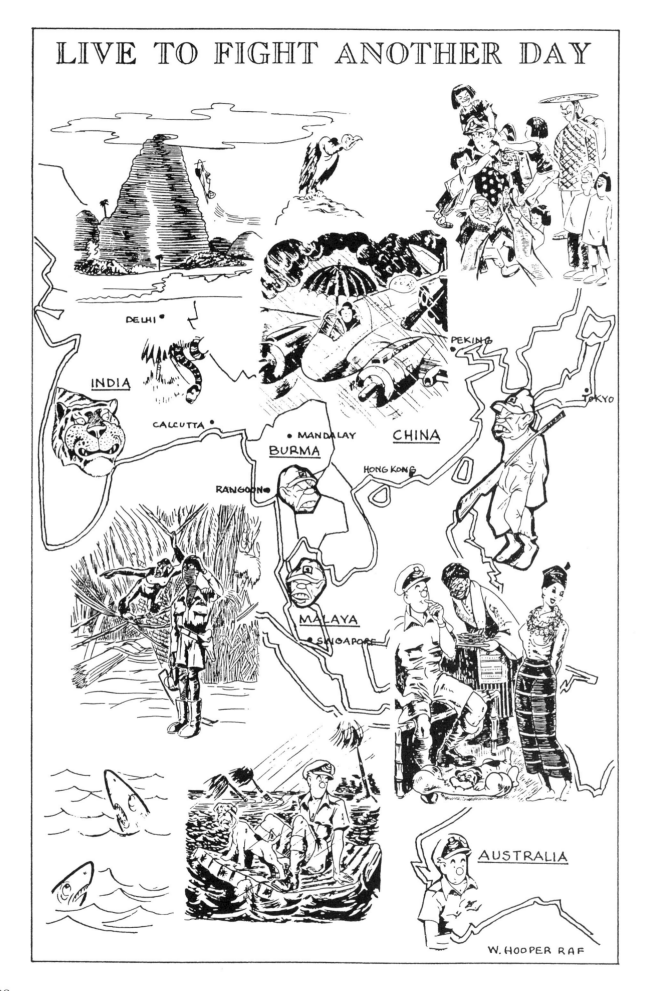

W. HOOPER RAF

Navigation was also a different problem in South-East Asia without the comfort of frequent radio beacons or convenient airfields to act as 'perches, Prunes, for the use of'. "In the UK P.O. Prune can quite happily lose his way or miscalculate his fuel and all it means is a pleasant and unexpected visit to a strange Mess with a can (*sic*) or so of beer thrown in. But if you miss your stopping place out East, it's not just a matter of putting down at another one ten miles further on. You may not be able to reach that next place at all with the fuel you have; so it's a question either of finding your destination or force-landing". The distances were great, there was a distressing absence of comforting landfalls and, on top of everything, the hills really were hills. Even flying at 10,000 feet didn't guarantee that you wouldn't bump into one. Flying in South-East Asia was further complicated by the enormously wide range of temperature that Aircrew might encounter; it was possible to take-off in snow and land in 110°F in the shade. "You should therefore be in a position to 'adjust your dress' accordingly", 'Tee Emm' commented. Prune, unable to comprehend the suggestion, merely let his copy fall to his side while he again mopped his brow with somebody else's pocket handkerchief.

"Down the Flights each ruddy morning,
Sitting waiting for a clue,
Same old notice on the Flight board,
Maximum Effort - guess where to!"

(RAF Anon - 1943)

OTHER TYPES

By 1940 a rapidly expanding Royal Air Force found itself made up of personnel from all over the world, including both Free and Occupied Countries. From the Dominions men had flocked to volunteer as Aircrew in the Royal Air Force and Canadians found themselves serving alongside Australians, New Zealanders and South Africans, each group adding its national characteristics to the flavour of a Squadron. Some Squadrons, particularly in Bomber Command, became either predominantly Canadian or Australian despite the eventual deployment of official Royal Canadian Air Force and Royal Australian Air Force Squadrons in Britain. In addition to the larger Commonwealth countries, volunteers came from just about any place that issued stamps bearing the King's head, including the Colonies and some of the Dependencies. Each man wore a shoulder flash denoting his nationality and so many different ones were spotted that, according to one apocryphal story, a certain NCO Air Gunner had his own made and went around proudly sporting 'Wapping' on his battledress blouse. As well those who sensed a duty to the Mother Country, there were the men of the Allied Air Forces of Poland, Czechoslovakia, France, Belgium, Holland, Norway, Yugoslavia and Greece and, prior to the USA entering the War in its own right, a group of Americans. Attempts were made to integrate most of these Allied airmen

Dutch Navy Air Arm with one of their Coastal Hudsons.

into the various Squadrons of the RAF, with the exception of those from the USA who, because of their prior allegiance to America, were only required to swear on oath that they would "serve faithfully and honourably for the War's duration", and were formed directly into what were to become known as the 'Eagle' Squadrons. Integration of the other Allies wasn't always easy; there were initial language difficulties and pride of nationality was impossible to suppress. Expediency made it simpler for nationals of like countries to be posted alongside each other in the same Squadrons, almost to the point of national domination, and very soon lobbying took place to create Squadrons that were unique to the nationality. The first and greatest pressures came from the Poles and from the French, each of whom made out the case that they should be regarded as part of an Allied Force, subject to RAF control, but based in Britain and fighting alongside the RAF against a common enemy.

The initial attempts to integrate the Poles into the RAF were not altogether easy. Their language was incomprehensible to most of the Allies, and to the public at large they sounded like Germans in RAF uniform. Most of them had escaped via Romania into France and eventually across to England. None

of them had experienced the comparative luxury of the 'Phoney War' and all had suffered in some way or another, including the tragic loss of families and comrades. The high standard of their training in Poland coupled with the need for experienced Pilots in Britain meant they were welcomed by the RAF and adopted into the Volunteer Reserve. General Wladyslaw Sikorski, Premier of the Polish Government-in-Exile and Commander-in-Chief of its Armed Forces, was very unhappy about this arrangement. There was a pact between Great Britain and Poland, and Sikorski argued vigorously for the establishment of an exiled Polish Air Force. After a long series of discussions with Churchill it was finally agreed that the Poles should be formed into their own Squadrons, both Fighter and Bomber. These would be self-governing in liaison with the RAF but to remain under its ultimate command. Principle was one thing but detail was another and it wasn't until the 1st of July 1940 that No. 300 Squadron 'Mazowiecki', (the first of 14 Squadrons to be manned by some 15,000 Poles that were to constitute the Polish Air Force-in-Exile), was finally formed. The Poles were completely self-supporting with their own training centres, their own ground staff, intelligence and administrative back-up. They wore a type of RAF uniform with their own Polish

101

"Have you read this month's 'Tee Emm'?"

Air Force badges and their aircraft were further identified with a small national red and white chequerboard square. As much as was possible they lived, ate and fought like Poles, honouring Polish traditions and festivals; and they were considered to be highly disciplined, impeccably trained and excellent fighters.

None of this concerned Pilot Officer Prune or 'Tee Emm' because although the Polish Air Force-in-Exile was well established by the time 'Tee Emm' made its debut, the Poles weren't eligible to receive it. The reason was rooted in the RAF's Air Intelligence Branch which had previously objected to the distribution of Intelligence Summaries to Polish Officers on the grounds that they "may be tempted in their correspondence abroad, quite innocently, to include information which might do us harm", and when the question of distributing 'Tee Emm' to the Polish Squadrons was raised at Air Ministry, a similar attitude prevailed. The problem was language. Only Poles could censor Polish and once the material was in their hands, no-one felt they had any control over its use. The problem was finally overcome by an approval to

translate 'certain' articles from 'Tee Emm' into Polish and to distribute these in an 'Official Use Only' category. This was rapidly followed by an agreement to distribute 'Tee Emm' itself but, because of its particularly English humour, it was not that well received. A request had originally been made by Group Captain L. Jarvis, Officer Commanding the RAF's Polish Depot, for permission to produce a Polish Monthly Digest. This was intended to be a 'Polish Tee Emm' but with less humour and some purely technical articles. After much soul-searching permission was finally granted in June 1941; but with a restricted paper allowance of 5,000 sheets per month. The first issue of 'Biuletyn Lotniczy' (Flying Bulletin) appeared in September 1941 and drew freely on 'Tee Emm's' content, including some redrawn versions of Prune illustrations. Always with an eye to the topical, Anthony Armstrong decided to use a Polish theme in an illustration headlining an article in that month's 'Tee Emm'. In fact, it was the first and last time either Anthony Armstrong or Prune had anything to do with the Polish Air Force-in-Exile; except to send them a regular copy of 'Tee Emm' for translation.

Every Christmas 'Tee Emm' resorted to this special front cover.

PLATE 7.

This front cover of 'Picture Post' was too good to miss so Anthony Armstrong
had it suitably embellished for reproduction in 'Tee Emm'.

PLATE 8.

LA R.A.F. EXPLIQUÉ
Par PERCY PRUNE P/O
À L'ASPIRANT LA PRALINE

Members of the 'Armee de l'Air' (French Air Force) who had made it to Britain before the capitulation of the French Government or had subsequently escaped from their Occupied or Controlled territories, sometimes with aircraft under the noses of the Germans, were viewed with suspicion on their arrival. Subjected to a period of interrogation and close scrutiny, each case was treated separately and it took some time before Military Intelligence would clear an individual to serve with the RAFVR. By the time General de Gaulle, following his call for all Frenchmen to fight on, had established his Free French Government in London, many former 'Armee de l'Air' Pilots were flying in RAF Squadrons. Unlike the Poles, General de Gaulle was unable to argue for these men to be formed into an exiled Air Force, but seizing on the precedent established by the Czechs with the formation of their own Squadrons, Vice-Admiral Muselier, Commander-in-Chief of the FNFL (Forces Nationale Francaises Libres), presented a case to Air Commodore D. Boyle, Director of Allied Air Cooperation, for the French to be treated in the same manner and brought together in one 'Free French' Squadron. Initially this proposal was met with enthusiasm, as was a

Commandant Duperier with French Naval Groundcrew on 340 Squadron.

AVEUX SPONTANÉS

similar proposal from the Belgians, and plans were laid with Fighter Command Headquarters for this to come into effect but it soon became evident that the French wanted more than just a Squadron with its own national identity. The first sticking point came with a French demand that they be subject to their own Military Code of Discipline and not beholden to RAF Law. This was unacceptable to Air Marshal Sir Sholto Douglas, Commander-in-Chief of Fighter Command; who insisted that not only would the Squadron remain under the operational control and disciplines of the RAF but it would be expected to provide its own (French) ground support personnel. He did, however, concede that, "the question of the responsibility for the internal administration of the Unit is one for General de Gaulle to settle". Effectively this meant that the French would be allowed to use their original 'Armee de l'Air' ranks and wear their own uniforms. The question of ground personnel was solved by a temporary release of Free French recruits from the French Naval Air Arm Squadron at Tahiti on their 'Chief's' understanding (Commandant Gayral) that these men would be returned, when requested. AM Douglas accepted this arrangement providing the men underwent a certain amount of retraining at an RAF OTU and

remained for a minimum period of six months; during which time the Free French HQ would recruit other Frenchmen to be trained to take their place. Also, the Squadron would have to fly under an RAF Commanding Officer until it had proved itself and a suitable French Commanding Officer had risen to the fore. Following a letter of confirmation from Sir Archibald Sinclair, Secretary of State for Air, to General de Gaulle setting down all the points and conditions that had been agreed, and insisting that they must be adhered to, No.340 Free French (Fighter) Squadron was formed at Turnhouse (13 Group) in November 1941 (the first of five French Squadrons).

In true Gallic manner the Free French or FAFL (Forces Aeriennes Francaises Libres) as the FNFL HQ referred to them, flew the 'Tricolore' wherever they were based, proudly wore their navy blue uniforms with gold bands of rank (albeit with the addition of RAF Pilot's 'Wings') and made a point of arriving at a new base in their Spitfires with a low-level pass in the formation of the 'Cross of Lorraine'. Utilising their rations to trade off with locals for different foods, they established a French-style cuisine in their French-style quarters and, apart from learning the English terms required for

CHRONIQUE DE L'ASPIRANT LA PRALINE

« Seriez-vous parent d'un certain Capt. Prune? »

Operations, stuck steadfastly to their own language. Their alliance with Fighter Command HQ remained

uneasy and attempts were continually being made by the Free French HQ to erode areas of RAF control - with a view to establishing the FAFL as an Air Force-in-Exile. It was hardly surprising that they should reject 'Tee Emm' which, by that time, was authorised for distribution to all 'Allied' Squadrons, and demand a publication of their own. The 'Bulletin des Forces Aeriennes Francaises en Grande Bretagne' didn't make its appearance until early 1943 after Commandant Bernard Duperier relinquished his command of No.340 (Ile-de-France) Squadron (see page 23: In the Beginning). He was assisted by Lieutenant 'Medecin' Berman of the FAFL and together they designed its format including the idea of 'Aspirant la Praline'. Its content, like the Polish Bulletin, was more broadly based than 'Tee Emm's'. It did, however, pay heed to visual content and, with a smart 'Bordeaux'-coloured cover, was produced as a small print run by 'Tee Emm's' printers. Anthony Armstrong never made any mention of the Free French as such, therefore neither did Pilot Officer Prune. And, they were left to their own devices aided by Prune's cousin 'Praline' who, despite his obvious lack of grey matter, didn't seem to be so accident prone (particularly with aircraft) as his RAF counterpart.

Pilots of the Free French (FAFL) receive decorations.

107

The Fleet Air Arm was yet another different group of people, in essence sailors who specialised in flying, but, more often, fliers who liked a connection with the sea. Their numbers were drawn from the Royal Navy, the Royal Naval Reserve and the Royal Naval Volunteer Reserve, as well as a number of Officers from the Royal Marines who had opted to take up flying duties. In addition, there were many Officers who had previously held Commissions in the Royal Air Force. The links with the RAF were strong, the Royal Naval Air Service having broken away from the Royal Flying Corps in 1914 only to rejoin again in 1918 to form the Royal Air Force. Then, in 1924, a Fleet Air Arm of the RAF was formed to operate under Admiralty control; its Pilots being Officers of the RAF as well as holding a Naval commission. This compromise of control lasted until 1939 when the Fleet Air Arm became part of the Royal Navy. In order to facilitate this changeover, the RAF loaned some 1,500 fitter/mechanics to the Navy and they served in the Fleet Air Arm but in RAF uniform. Elementary Flying Training was still conducted by the RAF for the Navy and the new influx of ratings destined to replace those NCOs loaned by the RAF, was being trained by the RAF at their Stations. Advanced Flying Training was conducted by RAF Officers and Sergeants but at Royal Navy shore based Air Stations.

With this sort of schizophrenic background it is little wonder that the Royal Navy made a special effort to imbue the men of the Fleet Air Arm with a solid sense of the Senior Service. After completion of their training at the hands of the RAF, Officers were sent to the Royal Naval College at Greenwich where they were treated to a solid dose of Naval tradition and pride. Efforts were made to instil the idea that for Naval Aircrew 'the sky was merely the roof of the sea'; but, in truth, most of them had no nautical experience at all. Even the deck-landing training was done ashore, with arrester wires rigged across a hard runway; and for those destined to fly fighters and torpedo-bombers, their first carrier

A critical moment for both Pilot and Deck-Landing Control Officer.

landing was often their first real taste of the sea. Their uniforms, both for Officers and ratings, were the same as the Royal Navy's except for the letter 'A' (Air) which was worn above the rank markings, and the Aircrew 'Wings' (Pilot, Observer, Gunner) were worn on the left sleeve. One tradition of the Royal Navy, the wearing of a 'full set' (moustache and beard) was frowned-upon if not forbidden in the Fleet Air Arm. For Aircrew this made good sense since it was important that the R/T oxygen mask was a perfect fit. Even so, a 'full set' was more maritime than aeronautical and requests for 'permission to grow' were few and far between.

The majority of aircraft flown by the Fleet Air Arm were either Naval versions of the RAF's fighters, strengthened to take the strain of arrester-hook landings (or catapult take-offs) and often with folding wings for under deck hangarage (Seafire, Martlet, Sea Hurricane), or carrier-borne torpedo-bombers like the Swordfish and various amphibians. The content of 'Tee Emm' therefore applied directly to the Fleet Air Arm as much as it did to the RAF and copies were automatically distributed. Since there was no special requirement for 'Tee Emm' to address itself to Fleet Air Arm Aircrew, no mention was made of the Service until, in mid-1943, a

request was made. The Commander responsible for Aircrew training in the Fleet Air Arm approached the Air Member for Training's Office to see if 'Tee Emm' could publish items specifically directed at Fleet Air Arm Aircrew in the same manner as it had for the RAF. The initial article, which was to be the first of many, dealt with the importance of strictly obeying the Deck-Landing Control Officer and set Anthony Armstrong the usual problem of having to rewrite the material in a light, digestible 'Tee Emm' form. To help with the Naval flavour, he added mentions of 'Ward Rooms', 'Pink Gins' and 'Plumbers' (this was the Navy's term for men dressed in boiler suits; ie. Groundcrew); but also alluded to Prune's exploits in the RAF. This was hardly satisfactory, since if it were to run as a regular feature, Anthony Armstrong needed his 'foil' to be first-hand. Prune was a member of the Royal Air Force and despite the fact that he served simultaneously in all Commands it would have been ridiculous to transfer him to the Fleet Air Arm as well. 'Sub-Lieutenant Swingit' was Anthony Armstrong's answer, quintessentially Naval with a 'full set' (despite the Fleet Air Arm norm) and a direct parallel to Prune but, to avoid any confusion, it was important that he should have different facial features. Bill Hooper's first drawing of 'Sub-Lieutenant Swingit' appeared in March 1944 and subsequently Prune appeared alongside him as if

Pilots of the Fleet Air Arm against a Seafire.

they were fellow travellers in dimwittedness. 'Swingit' ran for some nine month during which he became yet another established character in the Prune family. Towards the end of 1944, the Fleet Air Arm decided to publish their own monthly magazine, 'Flight Deck,' which addressed itself to all problems specific to Naval Flying. The FAA did, however, continue to receive regular copies of 'Tee Emm' which may have resulted in some duplication since there was no direct liaison between the two Editors. 'Sub-Lieutenant Swingit' didn't transfer, perhaps because he was a creation of the RAF. Certainly the Fleet Air Arm accepted 'Swingit' but never really adopted him as the RAF did with its Anti-Hero. The problem may have been the name. 'Swingit' lacked any possibility of being hurled in a derogatory manner and, after all, there really could be only one 'Prune'.

'Captains of the Clouds courageous,
Real or would-be heroes all,
Don't forget, in all your glory,
Pride precedes a nasty fall!'

(Tee Emm - 1943)

THE ORDER OF THE IRREMOVABLE FINGER

Towards the end of the first year of 'Tee Emm' numerous contributions were being sent in for consideration from even the farthest flung outposts of the Royal Air Force. Among these were accounts of 'Prunery' - all claiming to be true, although some were no doubt apocryphal. This alleged 'Prunery' had little to do with the main purpose of 'Tee Emm' but, like the titbits that Anthony Armstrong was writing around the main content of

the publication, added to its humorous flavour. Selected stories, particularly in the area of Flight Safety, could be used to teach by example of others' mistakes. In addition there were items in the weekly Accident Reports, reviewed by Anthony Armstrong, describing certain non-fatal incidents which could also be regarded as 'Prunery'. The question was how to present them in 'Tee Emm' to best effect? Some consideration was given to the idea of attributing them directly to Pilot Officer Prune and producing a whole-page drawing to illustrate the stories. This had possibilities but Anthony Armstrong saw greater merit in the idea of 'truth'; and providing the stories could be verified,

THIS MONTH'S PRUNERY

THE MOST HIGHLY DEROGATORY ORDER OF THE IRREMOVABLE FINGER (Patron : Pilot Officer Prune) has this month been awarded to S/Lt. (A) —— and Acting Leading Airman —— for Prolonged Finger Insertion in More Ways Than One.

Their aircraft had to make a forced landing in the sea, and much to S/Lt ——'s satisfaction, as Squadron Safety Equipment Officer, the "M"-type dinghy functioned correctly. Subsequently, however, it developed a small leak and since the only leak-stopper available was too big for the hole, the three occupants of the dinghy took it in turn to use their fingers till picked up two hours later.

It was later pointed out to them that a leak-stopper of the proper size was stowed inside the larger one they had rejected.

The M.H.D.O.I.F. has also been awarded to A. C. I. —— for Literally Gumming Up the Works.

This Air Mechanic, when refilling the coolant system of a Kittyhawk with Glycol, did so from a tin marked " Shellac Varnish," and seemed surprised to discover that it actually *contained* Shellac Varnish.

The M.H.D.O.I.F. has also been awarded to Wing Commander —— for Wanting to Get it Quite Clear.

While acting as Duty Wing Commander he asked the Ops. room about certain aircraft and was told they were not available as they were on a Daily Inspection. To this he replied : " O.K. And how often do these have to be done ? "

The M.H.D.O.I.F. has also been awarded to S/Ldr. —— (Tech. E.) for Knowing the Wrong Way to Put Things Right.

As Daily Servicing officer, he expressed considerable annoyance with a pilot who returned to base because one of his engines was giving an oil temperature in excess of the safety limit. He explained that the pilot should have flown into wind to cool it down.

The M.H.D.O.I.F. has also been awarded to Pilot Officer —— for Not Having a Clue.

This pilot landed at airfield " X " and told the Flying Control Officer he needed refuelling. When questioned by the Duty Engineer Officer he was unable to say whether his Spitfire was a XIV or a XVI ; whether his fuel was grade 100, 130 or 150 ; or what his maximum permissible boost was. All he knew was that he had been told to land at " X " airfield if short of fuel, but even this unexpected gleam of intelligence was dimmed by his almost immediately asking if " X " airfield was anywhere near.

---

as with the Accident Reports, they could be printed but with no names mentioned. The best could be selected and the perpetrators made the recipients of an award to be listed monthly. A precis of the incidents would then be published in the form of a mock citation. The well-known RAF phrase 'Pull your finger out!' (meaning roughly "Get a move on and don't be a damn fool" or "Stop daydreaming!

Buck up your ideas!"), which Anthony Armstrong had used in 'Tee Emm' on several previous occasions, offered promise. These stories were definitely cases where 'fingers hadn't been pulled out' and therefore Anthony Armstrong decided to create 'The Most Highly Derogatory Order of the Irremovable Finger' or 'M.H.D.O.I.F.' as it became better known. Bill Hooper set about designing an appropriate medal which was to hang from a ribbon described as 'narrow diagonals of light black against a dark black ground'. Laced with in-jokes, i.e. 'Putting up a black', etc., the medal depicted a gloved hand with an index finger 'inflexant non-movant' and bore the legend 'Faith et Blind Hope'. The M.H.D.O.I.F. (Prune was, of course, the Patron of the Order) made its first cautious appearance in March 1942 with just one recipient listed. Like Prune, it was an instant success and nominations for the award poured into 'Tee Emm's' office. Later the medal was modified with 'Dieu et Mon Doigt' (God and my Finger), codded from the Royal Coat of Arms, and a descending 'digit' forming the ribbon suspension ring. Such was the response from proposers of the award that, by the autumn, several recipients were being listed each month. The beauty of the anonymous citations was that it kept everyone guessing. More than one Aircrew member, who thought his 'Prunery' had

You are Old, Air Chief Marshal

"YOU are old, Air Chief Marshal," the young P/O said,
  " And your body's exceedingly fat,
Yet you fly thro' the air with the greatest of ease.
Pray what is the reason for that ? "

" The cause of this strange aeronautical grace,"
Said the Boffin, relating his powers,
" Was the arduous practice in cockpit routine
And learning instructions for hours."

" I know," said the P/O, " but answer me this.
I've seen you do circuits and bumps,
Yet you never come down with your undercart up,
Like me and the other poor chumps."

" You see," said the Marshal, with almost a smirk,
" It's habit, good training, and sense
To look round the cockpit at needles and tits,
Relax yourself ; never sit tense."

" Watch the pitch and the flaps and the mixture as well,
The airspeed and angle of glide.
It's so very much simpler to land on the wheels
Than prang on the belly or side."

" Watch the chap in the band box," the old boy next said,
" With his lights, and his lamps and his flags.
Pay regard to his gestures, his foibles and whims ;
Come in gently—no zigs and no zags."

" In my youth," said the Marshal, " I studied each word
That Flying Control put before me—
And avoided, thereby, those ridiculous prangs,
As frankly the stupid things bore me."

" Before taking off, get your maps—sign the book ;
The Form 700 as well.
Check the wind and the weather, the runway in use ;
Safety first—for you never can tell."

" I taxi quite slowly with caution and care,
And watch other aircraft about ;
It's foolish to argue with bowsers or trucks,
They have the last word, without doubt."

" I look after my helmet, my dinghy and 'chute—
It's true they belong to the King,
But friends who are corpses have proved more than once
To maltreat them's the craziest thing."

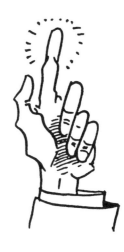

" I never take chances when close to the ground ;
And when clouds and high hills are about,
I use my R/T for all that it's worth
And keep all my fingers well out."

" Emulate me—young man—if determined you'd be
To grow old and get covered with rings,
Always bearing in mind, 'tis your chest—not your back
Should be used for displaying your wings."

By now our young P/O had had quite enough
And he started to yawn and to fidget. . . .
But he made up his mind that in future he'd try
To extract the proverbial digit.

---

slipped past unnoticed, wondered who had seen and shopped him – even though the incident cited may well have related to someone quite different. To be identified as a recipient of the Order was a grave punishment but many RAF Stations took up the idea on their own account. "They would have a replica of the insignia – a plaque showing the rigid index finger – made in the workshops and any wretched Officer of the Squadron who 'Put up a bad black' would be condemned to wear it in the Mess for a whole day to expiate his 'Prunery'. It was a sort of dunce's cap on a more exalted plane." Flight Lieutenant Adrian Bishop, a Transport Command Pilot, remembers: "The M.H.D.O.I.F. that I possessed was cast in lead and like the 'Tee Emm' design except that the obverse with the finger was inscribed 'Digit Inanus' and the usual two legends were on the reverse. The 'gong' was suspended from a black ribbon threaded through a brass ring set into the lead. This example had previously belonged to a PFF (Pathfinder Force) Lancaster Flight Engineer who had left it behind when he was posted, as in turn did I. But, I vividly remember an identical example hanging on the noticeboard in the crewroom of 44 Squadron at

Waddington in 1944 – suggesting that someone in Bomber Command was producing them to order."

Despite many readers' beliefs that the incidents cited were so ridiculous that they must have been concocted by 'Tee Emm's' staff, they were always true. Anthony Armstrong went to great lengths to verify the stories, and always from more than one source. Despite the recipients' names never being published, the details were always known and were held in files in 'Tee Emm's' office. In the 'Tee Emm' of August 1944 Anthony Armstrong reinforced the point by reporting an Air Commodore's complaint that one of the awards of the M.H.D.O.I.F. was a "bit far fetched." "'Sir,' we thundered indignantly, 'do you realise that each and every one of our Month's Pruneries are true?' He looked unbelievingly at us. Then he slank (sic) away. Or maybe we slank away – you know how Air Commodores can look. But it is true. All Pruneries are to the best of our knowledge genuine. In nearly every case we know the hero's Station; and in most cases we know names". The awards were made regardless of rank and Air Vice-Marshals down to Aircraftmen found themselves cited under

He then became quite fluent and conversational – having at last found out at what Station he had put down!". Anthony Armstrong could not resist writing a counterfeit rider to this and in the following issue of 'Tee Emm' he published a Note referring to the Group Captain: "We regret that it is not our policy in these awards to mention names. We can, however, publicly state that it was not any of the five Group Captains who at different times since the award have approached us secretly and said, 'I say, how did Tee Emm find out about me?' ".

The M.H.D.O.I.F. rapidly became an RAF institution and 'Finger' as a word on its own took on a special meaning. Chaps would refer to having a spot of 'Finger Trouble' and finger jokes abounded; with variations including 'Suffering from a Rigid Digit'. The popularity of the phrase 'Pull your finger out!', like most Service slang, soon found its way out into the public domain. And, despite further interpretations of meaning invested by the licentious, became an almost acceptable everyday phrase - although its use was not considered polite. In the early 1960s His Royal Highness Prince Philip, already famous for his forthright Naval approach, made the front page of

the dreaded black ribbon. One particular citation concerned a certain Group Captain and was awarded for 'Navigation!'. "On arrival at a Station, flying his own Moth, he was very guarded in all remarks to the Duty Officer and others, merely asking the way to the Mess. On arrival at the Mess he was still remarkably silent till on some pretext he managed to get a glimpse of D.R.O.s (Daily Routine Orders).

A bad case of 'Finger Trouble' with a Martinet advanced trainer.

several national newspapers when he addressed a group of city financiers at a Guildhall dinner. In criticising their reluctance to take action he told them directly to 'pull their fingers out'. This latter-day 'Royal Assent', undoubtedly for its original meaning, endorsed an acceptability for its use which nevertheless shocked many people at the time.

FINGERS AREN'T ALWAYS IRREMOVABLE

The old story of the armour to beat the gun, and then the gun to beat the armour has been repeated in the case of the barrage balloon. Explosive cutters are now fitted on the leading edge of our bomber aircraft, the general idea being that as the balloon cable slips into the cutter-housing it trips a trigger which explodes a cartridge. The cartridge, in turn, fires a chisel towards an anvil and frees the aeroplane by cutting the cable. All this is a Good Show.

On the other hand, it may turn out to be a Bad Show—that is, if it isn't after all a balloon cable which receives attention but an inquisitive finger.

For fighter aircraft are not fitted with this device, yet Fighter Stations quite often have our bombers dropping in on them, to refuel, or pass the time of day, or ask where they are, or simply have lunch. And A.C. Plonk—as a fighter air-craft mechanic and so not knowing much about bombers—may easily, while clambering over one such, stick his finger into the slot which was all set to receive a balloon cable. Result : removal of the finger.

Remember this, bomber crews who land at a Fighter Station. *You* may know all about your cable-cutters, but others may not. The finger may be that of an inquisitive Plonk, who wonders what the slot is for ; or of a quite innocent Plonk, unable to avoid in the dark something he knows nothing about. But the removal will be just as neat and expeditious. So warn all concerned ! Don't let them think—afterwards—that it was a practical joke in poor taste on your part.

If you *don't* warn them, it'll be your fault if a valuable mechanic is put out of action.

When the M.H.D.O.I.F. was first introduced it was with the blessing of Air Marshal Garrod who saw it as a logical extension of the use of Pilot Officer Prune. However, his tenure of the AMT's Office came to an end in April 1943 with a posting to Air Officer Commanding-in-Chief, India and his place taken by Air Marshal Sir Peter Drummond. An Australian by background, AM Drummond saw little sense in changing any of AM Garrod's successes and, appreciating that 'Tee Emm' was by then part of RAF folklore, left Anthony Armstrong to carry on much as he had been doing. There was rumour that some senior Air Officers disapproved of Pilot Officer Prune, of 'Tee Emm'

Air Marshal Sir Roderic Hill.

Commonwealth Air Training Plan (formerly EATS) with which AM Drummond had been heavily involved. His emergency successor, Air Marshal Sir Roderic Hill, arrived shortly before 'VE-Day' and at a time when the RAF was not only setting about a vast reduction in numbers but was determined to reimpose its pre-war standards of discipline and smartness. Within weeks of his arrival 'Tee Emm', although retaining its sometimes anarchic irreverence, began to pay heed to this new demand. AM Hill, posted from Commander-in-Chief, Fighter Command, believed in the old school technique of teaching by good example. Unable to change 'Tee Emm' overnight and with the certain knowledge that the end of the War in Europe would eventually spell out the demise of the publication, he merely strove to redress the balance; and, it was suggested to Anthony Armstrong that a 'Good Show' award be instituted as an antidote to the

M.H.D.O.V.O.

As Patron of the Most Highly Derogatory Order of the Irremovable Finger, Prune has lately been throwing his weight about too much for our liking. He keeps on bumbling into this office to show us the latest list of M.H.D.O.I.F awards, and to recollect with pride and admiration well-earned awards of past days, till he's ended by giving us the impression that there's hardly anyone in the R.A.F. who hasn't got his finger well and truly in for keeps.

Now, as we all know, that is not the case and so, as a counterblast to Prune, we are introducing a new Order to be awarded *not* for Pruneries, but for really Good Shows where fingers have been well and truly out.

We are calling it the **MOST HIGHLY DESIRABLE ORDER OF THE VACATED ORIFICE—M.H.D.O.V.O.**

and in particular of the M.H.D.O.I.F., regarding the whole operation as creating a sloppy and casual example which Aircrew might emulate. Whatever the arguments, AM Sir Peter Drummond defended 'Tee Emm's' record particularly in the costly area of Accident Prevention. His tenure of the AMT's Office was tragically curtailed in March 1945 when Churchill's famous B-24 Liberator transport 'Commando' disappeared somewhere on route to the Azores. On board with AM Drummond was the Under-Secretary of State for Air, his deputy and several other Air Officers on their way to Montreal for the Official winding down of the British

M.H.D.O.I.F. Citations were hard to come by since no-one was interested in reporting such incidents. At the same time 'Prunery' was being reported thick and fast and seeming to 'cock a snook' at the Most Highly Desirable Order of the Vacated Orifice, Anthony Armstrong stepped-up the number of citations for the M.H.D.O.I.F., giving the Order a full two pages.

Within months, the M.H.D.O.V.O. had been reduced to a simple 'Good Show' medal and continued, albeit occupying less and less space in 'Tee Emm'. The last awards of the M.H.D.O.I.F.

were made in February 1946 shortly before 'Tee Emm' was due to close. At which time there was an anonymous report of some joker being 'hauled over the coals' for sporting a black ribbon among his others on his 'Best Blue' uniform. The M.H.D.O.I.F. remains, although unlisted, as one of the more pertinent Decorations of World War Two.

"When the Court of Enquiry assembles,
Please tell them the reason I died,
Was because of an Irremovable Finger,
Which mucked-up my angle of glide!"

(RAF Anon - 1944)

VICTORY AND BEYOND

The 8th of May 1945 was officially declared VE-Day (Victory in Europe) and the final hard offensive by Bomber Command, Fighter Command and 2TAF (the 2nd Tactical Air Force), came to an end amid much rejoicing and high spirits. However, despite the well-earned self-congratulation and natural euphoria that attended this occasion, it still had to be remembered that we were fighting a 'World' war and Germany wasn't the only enemy. To a large extent the War in the East had been eclipsed by the immediacy of events in Europe. Reports from South-East Asia Command had taken a distinct second place in the National Press and although reports of the USAAF's successes in the Pacific were regularly published, the remoteness of their campaign held little drama compared with much less significant stories of success in Europe. The Air Ministry, via the Air Council and therefore the Air Member for Training, was aware of the dangers of 'believing we had won', and Anthony Armstrong was instructed to open the next issue of 'Tee Emm' (June 1945), under the heading 'Training Still Goes On', with an extract from a transcript of the Prime Minister's 'Victory in Europe' speech made on the 13th of May.

"We must never forget that beyond all lurks Japan, harassed and failing but still a people of a hundred millions, for whose warriors death has few terrors. I cannot tell you tonight how much time or what exertions will be required to compel them to make amends for their odious treachery and cruelty. We have received – like China so long undaunted – we have received horrible injuries from them ourselves, and we are bound by the ties of honour and fraternal loyalty to the United States to fight this great war at the other end of the world at their side without flagging or failing. We must remember that Australia, New Zealand, and Canada were and are all directly menaced by this evil Power. They came to our aid in our dark times, and we must not leave unfinished any task which concerns their safety and their future. I told you hard things at the beginning of these last five years; you did not shrink, and I should be unworthy of your confidence and generosity if I did not still cry, 'Forward, unflinching, unswerving, indomitable, till the whole task is done and the whole world is safe and clean.' "

In fact in late 1943, with the defeat of Germany on the cards and merely a matter of time, the RAF had started to lay plans for a long-range bombing force to fly alongside the US Navy in a combined offensive against Japan. Originally conceived as a force comprising some 40 Squadrons of specially modified long-range Lancasters intended to be operated out of various Pacific islands cleared by the US Navy and the US Marines, it underwent several changes of both strategy and aircraft types until plans were finally sealed by VE-Day. Drawing from Nos 5 and 6 Groups of Bomber Command, Lincolns (a further development of the Lancaster) were designated to replace the modified Lancasters as they become available. 'Tiger Force', as it had been officially named, was fully trained and ready to move out East when a change of tactics authorised by Harry S. Truman (the US President) resulted in the dropping of two Atomic bombs on mainland Japan. The devastation of this action caused an immediate surrender by the Emperor together with his Imperial Armies and the 15th of August 1945 was officially declared VJ-Day (Victory over Japan). For everyone including the RAF, 'Tee Emm' and Pilot Officer Prune, the war was truly over and had been won.

The Final Tally (Lancaster now preserved in the RAF Museum Hendon).

THE GEN THAT MATTERS

With victory under its belt the RAF, as did the other Services, basked in a natural sense of triumph and the feeling that the 'victors' could do no wrong. This lead to changing attitudes among Aircrew; and AMOs (Air Ministry Orders) and other 'Gen', which were vital to study when faced by the dangers of combat flying, lost their immediate significance. Added to this there was a general loss of purpose. The RAF was after all a fighting force and even though everyone was delighted that the war had been won, there was a general disappointment that there was no longer an enemy to fight. This led to a significant increase in 'Pruneries', and incidents of dangerous low-flying and other 'show-off' aeronautical feats began to rise. Ever mindful of the moment, Anthony Armstrong reasserted 'Tee Emm's' Flight Safety Campaign with a special emphasis on developing the right attitudes for Aircrew in a post-war RAF – and published a tale

of woe, based on a true incident, under the heading 'High Spirits Cost Lives':

"Prune takes off on a flight. We don't quite know what his briefing is, but for once he keeps rigidly to it, nor does he make any major boobs. A glow of self satisfaction spreads over him at this. He feels good. His spirits rise. He sings loudly in his cockpit, but luckily his somewhat bawdy warblings are drowned by the noise of the engine. Finding himself at this point over the sea – which, he understands, has no high ground for him to fly into – he ventures down to 50 feet or so. Still in the best of spirits and by now feeling rather martial, he pretends the war is still on and he is on a sortie to beat up enemy trawlers. In his present unnaturally righteous mood he actually resists the temptation to beat up an inoffensive British trawler, in the absence of German ones. A little further on he sees

something floating on the water, which will do instead. It's nothing important – just some sort of a buoy which can easily be replaced, and isn't much value anyway. He swoops on it and lets it have a burst. This being Prune's day, his aim is for once accurate and he sends it to the bottom. He then goes on his way in better spirits than ever. That night in the Mess his high spirits are infectious. He thumps the piano; he stands people beer; he talks about having his finger out for good and all and of turning over a new leaf. He shoots lines right and left. For he had a good day ... Out at sea, swearing men in a naval vessel are sweating to replace the buoy he has so light-heartedly destroyed. For it is an important one, marking an area of as yet unswept mines; and shipping, now no longer in convoys, has only these aids to rely upon for its safety. A little later the naval vessel itself strikes one of these mines. It is sunk and its crew lost. Back in the Mess the gay and irresponsible Prune, who believes he has for once had a boobless day, is still singing and drinking. Out in the sea good men are drowning. All thanks to Prune's high spirits".

Although demobilisation was planned to begin as soon as the war with Germany had been won, it took some months to swing into operation and followed a complicated formula of 'Release Groups' set out in a Government scheme. Faced with thousands of redundant Aircrew, the plan called for the retraining of those not yet due for release to take over the administrative jobs which had hitherto been done by peacetime solicitors, barristers, and business executives who volunteered for the RAFVR. To aid the process the RAF evolved

a series of courses on 'Administration' and 'Tee Emm' elaborated on their value and how it was proposed to deal with the surplus manpower in a steadily deflating RAF. "If you are going back to your old employer and he has promised you a better position on the strength of your war record, he will – perhaps unjustly, but certainly naturally – expect you to know more, not less, than when you left. He wants knowledge and ability, rather than D.F.C.'s and flying skills". A degree of uncertainty about

when demobilisation would take place, plus the clipped 'wings' of the majority of Aircrew, led to a slight lowering of morale. Certainly all those in the RAFVR expected to be demobilised within a year of VE-Day but, added to that was the problem of RAF regulars. Some, including those on Short Service Commissions, could reasonably expect to be retired, but there were those who wished to 'stay in' who were bearing War Substantive ranks and didn't know exactly where they would stand if they did remain. Also the Royal Air Force, with the new

By the end of 1945 it was already evident that the RAF was undergoing a dramatic change, not only in size of manpower but in terms of image. As with the prewar RAF, its successful future depended on a viable balance between the three Services (Navy, Army, RAF) and as in former years it was not only going to have to justify its existence but to compete for its share of a dramatically-reduced defence budget, which was political as well as strategic. In line with this philosophy a move was made to smarten-up the RAF and get back to the 'military'

WHY NOT STAY ON?

Newest machines, newest equipment, highly skilled men—these are wanted for the post-war regular air force. You who have done the job so well for so long are still needed to keep the Air Force at top pitch to face its great future responsibilities.

You need not commit yourself for a long period. You can join for 3, 4, 5, 6 or 7 years. If you are a regular you can extend your service to complete 12 years or you may be eligible to re-engage to complete 24 years and thereby qualify for a pension. Those of you who have served for 24 years may apply to continue in the Service for a further period.

For further details ask your Section Commander, Adjutant, Education Officer or Padre.

generation of jet aircraft now beginning to come into service, had to think of its own post-war needs and didn't necessarily wish to lose some of its top line personnel. Therefore it offered the possibility for certain VRs, in certain areas, to join the RAF 'proper', offering contracts of service of between 3 and 7 years while still allowing Regulars to continue with their normal extensions of service.

standards of the mid-thirties. "No longer is it thought 'tough' to be seen in the local immersed in Irvin jacket and flying boots, the necessary properties for Sergeant Flash-Alf's line shoots about his daring to the local populace. For the glories and glamour of 'being aircrew' and in the forefront of the battle must now be a thing of the past, and the reputation of the RAF in the minds of the public will be based

"But you fellows don't understand. *I'm air crew.*"

in the future largely on our appearance. Have you ever seen a policeman walking along with one hand in his pocket, his top button undone his greatcoat open with collar half turned up behind his ears, his helmet battered, greasy and askew, his neck adorned by a rather filthy spotted scarf? It must be remembered that the very word uniform means 'all the same' and not a mere general foundation on which to build your sartorial vagaries and whims".

'Tee Emm' entered 1946 with an uncertain future. Its original brief had fallen by the wayside in the light of Victory; its circulation had been reduced to a fraction as it still remained 'Official Use Only' and for listed Aircrew; and its style was somewhat out of step with the 'ideal' the Air Ministry was working to project. That 'Tee Emm' still performed a useful function there was no doubt; it was rather more its approach that was being questioned at Air Ministry level. And there was the question of 'Pilot Officer Prune'. It was one thing to have 'Prune' seen to be pranging a mass-produced prop-driven aircraft but quite another to let him anywhere near the vastly expensive Meteor and Vampire jet fighters which were to carry the RAF into the 'fifties. In fact Anthony Armstrong, as Squadron Leader A.A. Willis RAFVR, had already been demobbed, in line with the 'Release Scheme', in September 1945.

"My Demob. Group suddenly came up and I received a curt notice to take my bowler hat in a week's time. I told the authorities this and they said, 'If you go 'Tee Emm' will have to close down.' Though flattering, this was in a way true, as I had not only created the paper but run it for the whole of its life, and time would be needed to find another Editor. The alternative, however, was for me to commit immediate infanticide. So I said I didn't mind staying on for a few months while they made up their minds about the magazine's future. At the end of that time they said it had been decided that 'Tee Emm' must after all cease on my departure, no other editor being available. At this point I suddenly realised that there were now only three more issues needed to finish off the fifth volume. So I said that if they wished, I'd stay that three months longer and round off the 'Tee Emm Five Year Plan' with neat bow of ribbon, as long as they didn't mind my running it from home and only coming up to the Ministry when absolutely necessary. To this they kindly agreed, saying that provided 'Tee Emm' was on time and in the same style they didn't care what I did or where I worked".

What Anthony Armstrong didn't perhaps know at the time was that this arrangement suited the Air Ministry very well since it had by that time developed plans for the publication of a magazine to be entitled 'Air Clues' which was projected as a sort of successor to 'Tee Emm' but very much geared to the thinking of a post-war RAF. 'Tee

Emm' was set to publish its last edition in March 1946 and the first edition of 'Air Clues' which, like 'Tee Emm, would be under AM Hill (the Air Member for Training), was planned to follow a month or so later. The first issue of 'Air Clues' finally appeared in May 1946 and, following a 'Foreword' by AM Hill, its opening editorial made a point of stating that this new publication belonged to 'a new age of science and to a remodelled RAF', and spoke of 'the new RAF taking shape in the slipstream of the old'. Despite this there were many who were sad to see 'Tee Emm' coming to the end of its life, albeit that its term had run the course. Its humour and lively approach reflected, like the 'wartime spirit', a bond of friendship and a common purpose which was the essence of high morale. It was true that there was no real place for 'Tee Emm' in a post-war Air Force; neither could it have easily envolved to meet the needs. 'Tee Emm' always remained in the style in which it was conceived and, designed to 'suit the moment', had succeeded beyond the Air Council's wildest hopes. In fact, the eventual demise of 'Tee Emm' had been mooted in early 1944 to which a cryptic note to Anthony Armstrong from the then Air Marshal Sir Arthur Tedder read, "Dear Willis, Your briefing duly noted and understood *but* No Prune – no Tedder. Yours A.W. Tedder". Other signs of the beginning of the end began to show themselves and in King

George VI's Birthday Honours List oi June 1944, Anthony Armstrong, as Squadron Leader A.A. Willis, was awarded the CBE (Military Division) for his invaluable work with 'Tee Emm'.

H.G. MARTIN VIA C.W. CAIN

Although the die had finally been cast the outcome hadn't been unexpected and 'Tee Emm' had envisaged the demob of Prune as early as November 1944 with the announcement of the RAF's Educational and Vocational Training scheme. Under the title of 'How Will Your Civvy Suit Fit?', Anthony Armstrong explained what was fundamentally a resettlement plan, aiming to help personnel to cope with the outside world after a long period in uniform. "The object is to fit people for civilian life by giving them a background of knowledge and understanding of post-war problems. This will be done largely through discussions – for which they probably haven't had much opportunity during war time – helped out by lectures, broadcasts, films, handicrafts, clubs and so on. The general outline will be laid down by the Air Ministry, but the training will not be stereotyped; a lot will be left to the units to run themselves on their Stations, and in conjunction with the desires of the pupils themselves, aided by Education Officers and additional resident instructors. Educational Training will be mainly for those who want to improve their standard of education and their general qualifications for civilian employment. There will be, first, Primary Education for those not aiming as high as matriculation standard. It will lead eventually to a Service examination for the award of a RAF War Educational Certificate, which it is hoped will be recognised as a qualification for certain types of employment. Next there'll be Secondary Education, for those who wish to qualify

'But, dammit, I've flown a Spitfire and I've got my R.A.F. Certificate.'

for admission to a university and subsequent training for a profession. Again, there is an examination – the Forces Preliminary – success in which is recognised by the Universities as carrying certain exemptions for entrance, and which it is hoped will also be recognised by professional bodies. Lastly there will be Higher Education, for those already up to matriculation standard and wishing to continue studies at a higher level. The final part is Vocational Training. This, however, is only provided for those civilian jobs in which the prospects of employment are good. It is chiefly directed either to the improvement of the existing civilian qualifications of those already possessing them or who were in a similar job before the war, or to the conversion of Service qualifications to an appropriate civilian basis". To accompany this article on EVT, the first of many that were published throughout the last year of 'Tee Emm', Bill Hooper provided a series of illustrations projecting what 'Prune and his Crew' would be like in their 'Civvy Suits'. And, Anthony Armstrong concluded, by way of a parting gesture, "if you're going to get a civvy suit – as many of you are – do your best, while still in the Service, to see that it will fit you properly when you put it on".

IM NAMEN DES FÜHRERS
UND OBERSTEN BEFEHLSHABERS
DER WEHRMACHT
VERLEIHE ICH
DEM

PILOT OFFICER

P. PRUNE.

DAS DEUTSCHE KREUZ
IN EISERNE 2. KLASSE

HAUPTQUARTIER, DEN 1. APRIL 1942

DER REICHSMINISTER
DER LUFTFAHRT
UND OBERBEFEHLSHABER
DER LUFTWAFFE

REICHSMARSCHALL

DIE ERFOLGTE VERLEIHUNG
WIRD BEGLAUBIGT.

GENERAL DER FLIEGER

Always with an eye to the humorous Anthony Armstrong 'twisted the arm' of a contact he had in 'Captured Documents' out in Berlin and got him to supply an authentic certificate for the award of an Iron Cross Second Class. This was duly filled-in with Pilot Officer Prune's name and dated the 1st of April 1942 (his birthday). The story was then put about that the Luftwaffe had made the award to Prune for being responsible for wrecking more Allied aircraft than any German airman. The original certificate has long since disappeared but the above is a fair representation of how it originally looked.

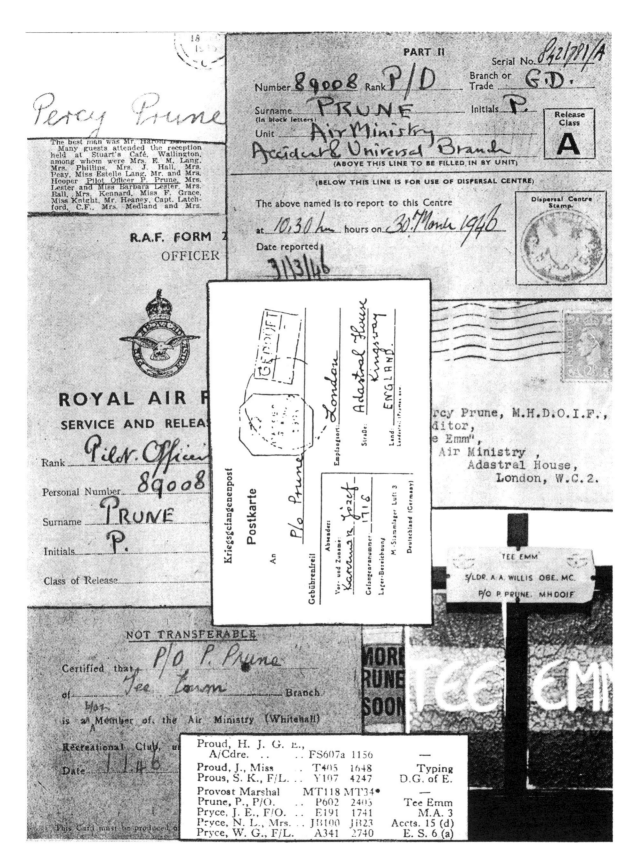

In the same vein Anthony Armstrong went to great lengths to support the idea that Prune actually existed in the Royal Air Force, getting him listed in the Air Ministry telephone directory, obtaining membership for him in various RAF Social Clubs, and obtaining Service Release papers to enable his demobilisation to take place – but not a pay record (that would have been fraud as almost certainly some pay clerk would have coughed-up). Prune received mail from all over including one from a Polish airman in a POW Camp stating, "I am missing news of you and am longing to see you!".

CIVVY STREET.

'The Times' of the 4th of March 1946, in its fourth column leader (which traditionally touched on lighter matters) announced, under the heading 'Mr. Prune', the imminent retirement from the Royal Air Force of one Squadron Leader Anthony A. Willis (better known as 'Anthony Armstrong'), Corporal W.J. Hooper ('Raff' the cartoonist) and their colleague a certain Pilot Officer P. Prune. Without mentioning the title of the classified publication 'Tee Emm' or its 'raison d'etre' or any of the subject matter it contained, 'The Times' proceeded to laud the value to the RAF of Prune's unerring inabilities and to offer hope for his future employment. "R.A.F. men will not hear unmoved the news that 'Pilot Officer Prune' is shortly to be demobilized, for he has played a considerable part in their wartime lives. Nor can the announcement escape a wider notice. The name and fame of this unhappy fellow who always did everything wrong have spread into the civilian life to which he is now returning, and many elderly and not particularly airminded people have learned enough from their offspring to know that the man who landed 'down wind' with his undercarriage up would infallibly be identified later as P/O Prune. Just as Laurel inevitably and invariably attracted the nearest pail

Open day at an RAF Station in 1946.

of whitewash onto the head of the devoted Hardy, so Prune, well meaning but weak, is the latest of a long line of characters in the world's literature to proclaim the truth of the proverb that 'He that will not be counselled cannot be helped' ". 'The Times' leader drew parallels with the use of 'high minded Billy Brown' and the 'active and benevolent Mr. Therm', both of whom appeared in posters of the period. But Pilot Officer Prune only existed in a visual sense to illustrate the points made by Anthony Armstrong in 'Tee Emm' and in truth his activities were more written about than visualised. Therefore Prune, together with 'Tee Emm' faded into the attics of most peoples' memories. That Prune made his mark in history is testified by the numerous passing mentions in various reference books and by his entry in the omniscient Oxford English Dictionary. For Anthony Armstrong, 'Tee Emm' and Prune represented just another 'period' of his colourful life and, with little reluctance, he returned to other projects, relishing the time he would now be able to spend in his beloved garden.

"Now there is nothing, not even our rank,
To witness what we have been;
And I am returned to my Walworth Bank,
And you to your margarine."

(Kipling – The Changelings)

PILOT OFFICER PRUNE – A BRIEF RESUME

"Percy was born, naturally enough, on April 1st 1922, at Ineyne Manor. At the age of six months, beginning as he meant to go on, he crashed his cradle, and within the next six months had crashed five replacements. As a child in the nursery he was so backward that at one time his parents weren't certain which way he was growing, or going. They went so far as to engage a mind specialist; but he soon threw up the job, saying he had nothing to work upon. Percy, however, did manage to grow up and went to school at St. Finga's, Herts, rising through the following years from 'new-bug', via 'Upper III B' to 'blood'. He left suddenly under a 10/10ths cloud, and in 1940 went up to the 'Varsity to Judas College. No sooner had he gone up than he was sent down and then called up. He was commissioned in the R.A.F. on the 1st April, 1941, his birthday, and funnily enough the date of the first issue of 'Tee Emm'. Since then he has been in Fighter Command, where he accounted for so many Spitfires that he was transferred to Bomber Command where he accounted for so many Lancasters that he was transferred to Transport Command, who wouldn't let him touch a single one of their planes, but had him transferred to the Air Ministry, where from sheer force of habit he promptly accounted for the three model aircraft hanging in this office. And in this office (Tee Emm) he stayed until his demobilisation".

Percy Prune

Pilot Officer, No. 89008.

Good-bye Chaps!
TEE EMM
You've Had It!

Vol. 5 No. 12 and final !   March 1946

for official use only.